Plenty Ladylike

CLAIRE McCASKILL
with TERRY GANEY

Simon & Schuster
New York   London   Toronto   Sydney   New Delhi

Simon & Schuster
1230 Avenue of the Americas
New York, NY 10020

First Simon & Schuster hardcover edition August 2015

SIMON & SCHUSTER and colophon are registered trademarks
of Simon & Schuster, Inc.

For information about special discounts for bulk purchases,
please contact Simon & Schuster Special Sales at 1-866-506-1949
or business@simonandschuster.com.

The Simon & Schuster Speakers Bureau can bring authors to
your live event. For more information or to book an event contact
the Simon & Schuster Speakers Bureau at 1-866-248-3049 or visit
our website at www.simonspeakers.com.

Interior design by Lewelin Polanco

Manufactured in the United States of America

10 9 8 7 6 5 4 3 2 1

Library of Congress Cataloging-in-Publication Data

McCaskill, Claire.
  Plenty ladylike / Claire McCaskill, with Terry Ganey.
      pages cm
  Includes bibliographical references and index.
1. Legislators—United States—Biography. 2. United States. Congress.
Senate—Biography. 3. United States—Politics and government—21st
century. 4. Political culture—United States—Anecdotes. 5. Women—
United States—Social conditions—21st century. 6. Women politicians—
Missouri—Biography. 7. Auditors—Missouri—Biography. 8. Missouri—
Politics and government. I. Ganey, Terry. II. Title.
  E176.M125 2015
  328.73'092—dc23
  [B]
                              2014047549

ISBN 978-1-4767-5675-2
ISBN 978-1-4767-5678-3 (ebook)

To my mother and father

who made me believe that ambition, strength, confidence, opinions, and yes, bossiness were all ladylike

Contents

CONTENTS

Plenty Ladylike

CHAPTER ONE

Blonde Ambition

S treet after street, door after door, I walked and knocked. "Hello, I'm Claire McCaskill, and I'm an assistant prosecutor. I'm running for state representative, and I'd appreciate your vote."

I was twenty-eight years old, single, a renter with no money or political organization backing me up. It was 1982, and I was a young prosecutor with courtroom experience who was comfortable making a case and doing hard work. When I ran for my first political office, a seat representing part of Kansas City in the Missouri House, people told me I needed to knock on doors. I knocked on 11,432 of them.

While I remember many of these encounters, one has replayed itself in my head hundreds of times over the years. It was dusk on an early summer evening as I approached a small Tudor in a modest neighborhood. I'd been knocking for several hours by the time I reached this house. A man in his upper-middle years opened the door, and I rattled off my greeting. He looked me over slowly, up and down, and said, "You're too young. Your hair is too long. You're a girl. No way are you tough enough for politics. Those politicians in Jeff City'd eat you alive. Go find yourself a husband."

And he slammed the door in my face.

I won that race—and I kept on running for the next thirty years.

From a very young age, I was driven. In school I spoke up so much I earned the nickname "Motor-mouth McCaskill." I didn't want to just get A's; I wanted to win every spelling contest. I didn't want to be just a cheerleader; I wanted to be captain of the squad. Until I got to college I didn't realize that such drive wasn't always socially correct. My parents had done an amazing job of protecting me from a very dangerous point of view: that women should not be ambitious.

My mom, Betty Anne McCaskill, emphasized early on that women can do anything men can do. She refused to let me and my sisters, Anne and Lisa, get a Barbie, Queen of the Prom board game when we were young. To win the game you had to get a dress and a boyfriend and go steady. "Dumb game. That is not how you win anything," she told us. While she never discouraged marriage, she and Dad both reinforced the need for us to first be self-sufficient. In that sense, my parents were way ahead of their time in stressing independence. My dad's words still ring in my ears: "You can't find happiness with someone else until you are happy with yourself." My dad, Bill, gave me the gift of incredible respect for a sense of humor. Even while I was ambitious, the people in my household taught me not to take myself too seriously. And as the most important male figure in my life, my father also gave me permission to be bossy and opinionated.

When I was in high school, I encountered my first situation

where I had to choose whether to go along and be popular or to speak out even though I risked alienating some of my friends. The social sorority to which I belonged had always used popularity as the only measure for inclusion. I took the risk of saying that it might be a good idea to look at grades and school activities and maybe work for a little diversity if we were really focused on service as much as prestige. I felt strongly about this, and it hurt when my friends turned against me. That evening, as I was crying in my room, Dad quietly told me to snap out of it. He asked me to choose whether I wanted to be a leader or a follower, pointing out that followers never got their feelings hurt, but leaders always do. He told me one of his corny jokes and made me laugh. That was the year that Dad gave me John F. Kennedy's book *Profiles in Courage* for Christmas.

Each year Dad encouraged me to enter the American Legion speech contest at West Junior High School. Though I made the finals in seventh and eighth grade, I never won. The contest required memorization of the speech, no notes allowed. One of those years I had the traumatic experience of forgetting my speech in front of the entire student body. Part of me wanted to sit out the competition in ninth grade, but a bigger part wanted to win. Dad and I talked about it and decided that my topic for this last try needed to be something I felt strongly about. I chose to give a speech about the Ku Klux Klan. He had me research the KKK, and we decided together that their offensive and repugnant oath would be a dramatic beginning to the speech.

I can recall exactly how I felt standing alone at the podium, and I remember where Dad was sitting. And I can still feel the surge of adrenaline when, as I opened with those sickening words of allegiance to racism, I felt the connection with the audience and the incredible high when the thunderous applause came at the end of the speech, when I closed with the Pledge of Allegiance. Later Mom told me that when they announced me the winner, Dad was crying.

It was probably around that time that I started talking about being Missouri's first woman governor.

If you wanted to predict where I might end up, there are some good clues in a series of episodes that took place during my junior and senior years at Hickman High School in Columbia, Missouri. I had been a cheerleader all through junior high and until my senior year at Hickman, when they brought in professional judges to pick the team and I didn't make it. It was as if the roof had fallen in on my life. My younger sister, Lisa, can still recall coming home and finding me sprawled across the bed, sobbing, mascara running down my face. What a comedown. What a catastrophe.

To make up for losing my cheerleader's spot, I launched a secret comeback by running for Hickman's homecoming queen. It was a stealth operation because nobody really "campaigned" for the honor. The football team chose the queen, usually the girlfriend of one of the team captains. I figured out that all the votes from the linemen and the second- and third-string players were being taken for granted, and I methodically identified all these players and their girlfriends. Then I quietly began to reach out to them. I paid them special attention, did favors, arranged dates, and went out of my way to show I cared. I did it subtly and slowly for months.

At first the plan was all about me. But I came to learn that I really liked the people whose votes I was courting. They became my friends, and I started to believe that I was actually giving them some input into a process they never had before. The following winter I wore the homecoming crown, and although I wanted others to believe I won because I was popular, in fact I had carried out an effective political operation by identifying a constituency and working hard to gain its support. For years afterward I kept to myself what I had done, talking about it only with my closest friends. I'm still slightly embarrassed to admit that I campaigned for homecoming queen, but it's important for women to own being strategic. To this day I remain friends with some of those linemen on the football squad.

Losing my cheerleading spot helped me in the long run. The only salvation I could find at that time was when I became Pep Club president and, at my dad's urging, joined the competitive speech and debate squad. I had to learn how to speak on any topic I was given only moments before walking into the room for the tournament. It was a frightening thing to do, but I remember hitting my stride during the third contest and thinking, *I can do this*. That confidence has come in handy countless times in the courtroom, on the campaign trail, and on the floor of the U.S. Senate. I soon discovered that other students were warming up to me now that I had been brought down a notch or two from my cheerleading pedestal. I realized vulnerability can be an asset.

The day after I graduated from Hickman High School, I packed my beat-up Chevy Nova—bought with money I made working as a clerk at a fabric store—and took off for a job bussing tables at the Lodge of Four Seasons at the Lake of the Ozarks. Every summer throughout college I worked as a waitress at the Lodge, located about an hour from Columbia and the University of Missouri. You learn a lot about people when you wait on them. You learn how to communicate and how to calm people down when they're upset or frustrated, and you learn that giving people information in a friendly manner can produce great results. That is another important skill in politics.

Before I graduated from high school, I made up my mind that I was going to law school. I pursued a political science degree at the University of Missouri and concentrated on getting good grades. I set goals for myself, and I'd often lie awake at night plotting out how to achieve them. I considered each step that would be necessary in the process and identified allies. Sometimes my ambition surprised me. As a freshman I pledged one of the school's most prestigious

5

sororities. I was the first woman to chair the university's homecoming gala. I became a football hostess, a job in which you help recruit athletes. While landing the hostess position depended partly on looks, you also had to know enough about football to answer their questions and show you understood the game. You had to know the difference between a tight end and a linebacker because when you're meeting with a potential recruit it is important to make him feel welcomed and needed, and knowing about his job as a football player was part of that.

Many years later, Anne Loew, one of my sorority sisters, talked about how, though it might have looked easy, I had put a lot of work into getting to where I wanted to be. "We'd walk into a party and all I'd want to do was grab a beer and have some fun," she said. "But then I'd notice Claire working the crowd. She seemed to have an unerring ability to single out the most important people in any group—whether students or professors—and concentrate on them. It was a challenge to her to win them over. It didn't matter if they were her enemies. Claire would be there, smiling and chatting. 'Why have an enemy,' she'd say to me, 'when you can have a friend?'"

Over time Anne learned that I was working on a long-term plan—that each step forward was getting me closer to a specific goal. Jill McDonald, another friend from those days, didn't like me at first because I seemed a little too opinionated, a little too pushy. But later she came to see those traits as independence. "Despite her ambition, in some ways Claire really didn't care what other people thought of her," Jill said. "In her personal life, she did what she wanted. In that area she never compromised to achieve anything, and yet somehow she still came out all right, though there were people who came to hate her for that attitude. Back then there were still lots of men and women around campus who wanted her to be just another meek sorority type. Claire just said 'to hell with them.'"

More valuable to me than my political science classes were the outside experiences that came with them. For example, in 1974, when I was a junior, I conducted research for one of my professors, David Leuthold, by attending the Democratic Midterm Convention in Kansas City. Warren Beatty was there as a delegate, and it was interesting to me to see how much more attention the movie star received than the well-known feminist icon Bella Abzug. One summer I took a comparative government course at Georgetown University and interned in the office of Congressman Jim Symington of Missouri. My most valuable learning experience outside the classroom came with an internship in the Missouri Legislature in Jefferson City. That was an unsettling initiation, an introduction to something they never discussed in civics class. It was 1974, and I went to work in the office of State Representative Sue Shear, a Democrat from the St. Louis County suburb of Clayton. It was the first time I experienced moments of being very uncomfortable as a young woman surrounded by lots of men.

There were inappropriate things said to me and inappropriate behaviors that made me very uneasy. Representative Shear's office was on the ground floor of the capitol, so I began my internship spending lots of time on the nearby elevator, as I was sent on errands to the upper floors of the building. One day I ended up in the elevator with two older male legislators and one of their assistants. They began asking if I liked "to party" and then tried to get me to come to one of their offices for some drinks. I felt trapped. For the rest of the internship, I took the stairs.

I also watched in horror at the way Sue's colleagues marginalized her. They were patronizing and dismissive. When she was elected in 1972, she was the first woman to be recruited and supported by the Women's Political Caucus in Missouri. There were only a handful of women in the Missouri Legislature then, and Sue was a crusader. She was willing to fight anyone anytime over the issue of women's rights. But because she was sounding one note almost exclusively, she wasn't taken as seriously as many of her women colleagues. With the determination of a bulldog, she wanted to pass the Equal

Rights Amendment, though she didn't make much headway. So although I loved and admired her, watching her made me realize that sheer determination and focus alone are not going to win the day. The Missouri Legislature never did pass the ERA.

There were women legislators who would try to be one of the boys, making deals and cracking dirty jokes. Judy O'Connor from northern St. Louis County won a special election in 1971, filling the seat that had been held by her husband, who was killed in a car accident on his way to the state house. Winnie Weber from House Springs in Jefferson County, known as "the life of the party," had won her seat in 1970. Observing my female colleagues in the Missouri House in the eighties made me realize that self-effacing humor combined with a passionate focus on substantive issues could be effective, whereas either one in isolation, not so much.

A year after my internship with Shear, in 1975, I graduated with a bachelor's degree in political science and immediately entered law school at the University of Missouri in Columbia. I got accepted elsewhere, but I went to Mizzou because I knew that being part of the network of lawyers in Missouri would help me more with any future political campaigns. I became close to many of my classmates, including David "Doc" Limbaugh, brother of the future conservative radio celebrity, and David Steelman, who would later marry Sarah Steelman, one of the three candidates who sought the GOP Senate nomination to oppose me in 2012. I had serious political differences with Doc and David, but it would not be the last time that I made fast friends with those who held opinions that were different from mine.

I didn't like law school very much. I liked the trial-related courses, but property, trusts, wills, and tax law really didn't engage me. Everyone was very competitive, so there was a lot of one-upmanship and talk of high-salaried jobs with big law firms. As a result I didn't spend a lot of time hanging around the school; instead I took a job as a waitress in Columbia. When I studied, it was usually at my apartment or on my work breaks. My job gave me perspective, because when everyone else was stressing out over law school, I was trying to figure out whether the order I turned in for a medium rare steak had been correct.

After graduating from law school in December 1977, Kansas City was my destination. I chose it because I didn't know anybody there and no one knew *me*. I wouldn't be "Bill and Betty's daughter." I wanted to make it on my own. I had grown up for the most part in Columbia and had been a "townie" while going to school, and it was time to leave. My law school grades were just average. I applied at some law firms without success and ended up as a research attorney for the Missouri Court of Appeals in Kansas City. Unlike being a law clerk for a judge, the research staff did legal work for the entire court. It was grunt work; the research attorneys occupied the lowest rung on the ladder in the hierarchy of the court of appeals. Stuck at my desk in the stacks on the eleventh floor at the Jackson County Courthouse, it seemed like I was going nowhere. And I was bored, so bored that a judge once caught me napping on a hideaway couch.

The job didn't pay well, and I had thousands of dollars in student debt. So the following spring, I used vacation time to go to California with the express purpose of getting on a game show to win money to pay off some of my student loans. Like many others, I had watched game shows on television and thought, *I can do that!* By then my friend from college, Jill McDonald, was living in LA, and I knew I could have her couch during my visit. When I got out there, I interviewed for several shows, took the tests, and went through the paperwork. Eventually I was accepted for a show called *High Rollers*. Alex Trebek was its master of ceremonies. In this game two participants were given multiple-choice or true-false questions, and if you answered correctly you would roll the dice that could lead to prizes. They taped five segments in one day, and I was champion on four of them. I won $37,000 in cash and prizes and a trip to Italy.

"She won everything from a fur coat to a bedroom set," my mom said later. "It was just ridiculous. A lot of it ended up in my base-ment, since she lived in a small apartment in Kansas City, while she worked at selling most of it to pay off her student loans."

I didn't use up all my luck on *High Rollers*. Still miserable as an appeals court research attorney, I set up interviews at the Jackson County prosecuting attorney's office and with the public defender. I longed to be in a courtroom, and I knew that those two offices offered the best chance. Very few lawyers actually get into a real courtroom to practice except in the area of criminal law. Luckily the prosecutor's interview was first; I was hired on the spot. Work in the prosecutor's office was far superior to work in the public defender's office when it came to building a résumé for the political offices I planned on seeking. I worked there for four years, and to this day I'm still using what I learned from that period of my life.

When I started that job, there were no women in the office with whom I engaged on a professional basis other than the secretaries and the women who operated the elevators. There were a couple of female police detectives, but all of my colleagues were men and all of the bosses and the judges were men. I had to decide every day whether I was going to rock the boat over sexist behavior or was going to keep my head down and earn respect by being a top-notch trial lawyer. I generally chose the latter course.

In one of the first major cases that I was assigned, I found my-self up against Larry Gepford, the former elected Jackson County prosecutor. I was nervous. This man had been the boss of my office, knew everyone in the courthouse, and was close friends with all the judges. When it was time to take a deposition of one of my witnesses, I walked into the conference room, where Mr. Gepford was already seated comfortably, with the court reporter nearby. He looked at me and said, "Honey, get me two yellow pads, a pencil, pen, and a red marker. Also get me a cup of coffee while you are at it." I had to make a split-second decision: Do I confront him right now and set him straight that I am neither his secretary nor his honey, or do I deal with it another way? I graciously got his pads, pencil, pen, and coffee, and we did the deposition. But for the next six weeks I worked my tail off preparing for that trial, and when the verdict came in guilty with the sentence that I had asked for, it was especially sweet. He told my boss that I was a "tiger in the courtroom." That felt good, much better than the momentary satisfaction of telling him off.

While many of my colleagues in the prosecutor's office became good friends, and while most of the judges I appeared in front of were honorable and supportive, there were a few very crude characters. Referring to me and another woman who later joined our office, one told his buddies, "I don't think it's fair to have two hot women in the courtroom." One judge kept badgering me to go out with him. He would call me to his chambers whenever I had a case before him, and I learned to always bring one of my colleagues with me. I eventually had to ask my boss to help me avoid assignments in his courtroom.

At the beginning I was doing food stamp fraud, then they had me prosecuting sex crimes: child abuse, rapes, and assaults. I lost one of my first cases because I failed to nail down a technical point. It was a rape case; the victim had gone home with a man from a bar, and he had brutally raped her. I failed to establish beyond a reasonable doubt the identity of the perpetrator. I glossed over that point because it seemed obvious to me, and when the jury came back with a "not guilty" verdict, I felt as though I had allowed the criminal justice system to assault the victim all over again. *How could they have done this?* I wondered. *What would I tell the victim?* I was so upset that I started to lunge toward the jury as they were filing out, wanting to confront them, but one of the other lawyers in the office, a more senior prosecutor, held me back and said, "You need to take a deep breath and get control of yourself."

One of the most difficult conversations I've ever had was the one I had with that victim when the trial was over. For many years afterward, she sent me a card each Christmas. They were precious to me; with each one she was forgiving me. I learned an important lesson from that trial: pay attention to detail, be prepared, and never take anything for granted.

Another rape case has stayed with me. I was a very junior prosecutor, sitting in a conference room in the law library where we would meet once a week to go over the trial docket for the following week. I was the only woman in the room, and a rape case was on the docket. The trial docket supervisor said, "I don't think we can take it to trial. The defense is that she consented. She's single, was out at a bar, and had an IUD in. Sounds like a loser." It was as if a bucket of cold water had been poured over my head. This was one of those critical moments: *What do I do? Do I speak up? If I do, what happens? And if I don't, what does that mean? How do I advance an opinion in a way that is most effective and remains true to my principles but doesn't hurt my career?* I was a single woman on the pill. If I got raped that night, was my office not going to take the case because of that?

I didn't say anything at the meeting, but afterward I went to the docket supervisor and told him, "I think you guys need to think this through. This is not good. You can't prejudge the victim based on whether she was using birth control." Later he acknowledged my point, saying something like "I never thought of that."

Over time the sexual assault cases began to eat at my emotional health. I told my bosses, "You know, I deal with the worst form of humanity day in and day out, and it is beginning to impact how I view the world and how I view men. Every man is beginning to look like he's a creep that's committed some horrific sexual assault." I began looking around for other opportunities to advance within the office.

In 1980 the Law Enforcement Assistance Administration awarded a grant to help prosecute arson for profit. It included money for a new position, a full-time special arson prosecutor, and I went after that job. An arson case is very difficult to prove; it involves a lot of science and circumstantial evidence. And while you might establish that a fire was caused by arson, it's very difficult to prosecute the perpetrator. There are usually few or no witnesses, and you have to dig through a lot of tedious financial stuff. It's not exciting, and prosecutors usually shy away from cases that are difficult to win.

I lobbied hard and successfully for the new position. While I recognized it would be tough to make circumstantial cases, the job was a big break. It came with a substantial raise, and the grant also paid for me to receive specialized training in arson's causes and origins. That gave me expertise and credibility, making me more marketable down the road. Insurance companies want to hire lawyers who know how to prove arson because they don't want to pay claims to people who have burned down their buildings.

The grant also gave me the ability to shape the position into something more than just handling a criminal caseload. I reached out to the community and brought in insurance agents and firefighters and others who deal with arson. We established an Arson Task Force, which put police, firefighters, and the insurance industry at the same table, talking and cooperating. We began promoting community awareness, which allowed me to give speeches and presentations throughout the state. In the end we achieved one of the highest conviction rates for arson in the country while filing the kinds of cases that previously would have been declined by busy, overwhelmed prosecutors. Eventually I traveled around the country, helping to train other prosecutors on arson.

Prosecuting the cases generated favorable publicity. On April 22, 1981, the *Kansas City Star* ran a story with the headline "Arson Pays? Not against This Prosecutor," with a photo of me pulling on firefighter's boots. The story recounted how I had tramped through the ashes of an arson-caused fire that destroyed an apartment building and killed six people. It pointed out that in the previous year the new arson squad had filed 101 cases, compared with seventy during the previous four years combined. Captain Billie T. Moran, the commander of the Kansas City Police Department arson control unit, said the squad's arrival had increased the number of arson convictions. "It's really a very difficult crime to solve and prosecute," Moran said. "If nothing else, we are proving it can be done and I think with a great deal of success."

By this time I had become a trial team leader, supervising three or four other attorneys handling felony prosecutions. One of those who joined my team in 1981 was Louis Accurso, who would become my lifelong friend, law partner, political supporter, and godfather to one of my children.

"She taught me how to use the right degree of sarcasm in cross examining a witness," Accurso said later. "She would do a 'You mean to tell me?' and you could see she had the witness on the ropes. I don't think I've ever seen it in another female trial lawyer, and that's probably one of the hardest jobs on the planet, outside of being a single mother. She had to find a way to be aggressive without acting like a man. And she never acted like a man; she always acted like a very classy, well-spoken woman, and she never hid her femininity; she always dressed really well, and she used to have really long blonde hair, and she tossed it when she needed to during a trial."

Robert Duncan, one of the Kansas City area's most distinguished criminal defense attorneys, once calculated that he and I had faced off eight times. "She's not the least bit afraid to go straight for the throat," he said. We tangled over the celebrated case of a restaurant fire at Gordo's Lounge, which occurred late one night in 1978. Three times we went to court; the first trial ended in a hung jury, the second, a mistrial, and the third time, a conviction. There was no question that the fire had been set. The building had been soaked in paint thinner and gasoline; the restaurant was locked and there was no sign of forced entry; and the property owner had recently doubled his insurance. Still, it was difficult to prove who did it. The state supreme court later upheld the conviction, and the case became a landmark for circumstantial arson cases and impeachment of witnesses, and is still cited in legal opinions and briefs.

 I taught prosecutors on my trial team to hunt for details. For example, if a house has burned down suspiciously, where were the pets? Where were the children? Did the people who owned the home behave in a different way during the time leading up to the fire? In the Gordo's Lounge fire, I noticed in the photos of the debris that a large and very expensive cut of meat was still sitting on a charred table in the kitchen. During the trial, I didn't mention this photo when I entered it into evidence, but when I summed up the case for the jury, I asked, "Is it reasonable to believe that a restaurant owner who intended to open again the next day would just walk out and lock up, leaving meat of that value to rot?"

The attention the arson squad generated brought me assignments across Missouri. Soon I found myself in Joplin, prosecuting a woman accused of murder and arson in the death of her husband. There were odd details in that case. For example, the night of the fire, which was in a rural area, the wife talked to the firefighters and told them about what had happened and her "innocent" activities that evening, complete with tears and expressions of grief. I noticed that in her statement that night she had gone out of her way to talk about the gas can on the basement steps. She told the firefighters that she had realized the cap was not on the can after the fire had broken out upstairs in the house, and that she had secured the cap before she escaped the fire so it "wouldn't make it worse." *Why would she go out of her way to point that out, unless she was worried about her fingerprints on the gas can?* I wondered. I then checked the records and learned that the power went out in the house as the fire broke out. In the darkness she would not have been able to see whether or not the cap was secure. She was lying. Her fingerprints were on that can because she had used it to pour gasoline in the doorway of her bedroom where her husband was sleeping, and then poured it down the stairs to the first floor of the house. She then left the can on the basement stairs, lit the fire, and waited for the fire department to arrive, feigning horror that her husband was burned alive while trying to escape through a bedroom window that was too small for him to get through. Exposing that lie was key to unraveling her defense. The jury found her guilty of manslaughter.

One of the things that disturbed me during my earliest years in the Jackson County prosecutor's office was the fact that employees, staff, attorneys, nearly everyone who worked there was expected to contribute money to the prosecutor's reelection campaigns. In politics it's called a "lug." Someone representing the campaign would come around asking for donations. Most of my coworkers didn't make that much money; my own starting salary was less than $13,000 a year. In those days I was getting around in my second old Chevy Nova, which was so rusted you could see the ground through a hole in the floor. I was so offended at being expected to contribute that I made up my mind I would never solicit a campaign contribution from someone who worked for me.

In 1981 Ralph Martin was succeeded as prosecutor by Albert Riederer, and for the next three decades Albert was at various times my boss, my friend, my mentor, my political rival, and my counselor. He helped launch my political career, but he also short-circuited it. Sometimes we collaborated on legislation, sometimes we fought in public, and sometimes we competed for the same office. Our relationship swung up and down, but in the end we never let our rivalry get in the way of our friendship.

When Albert tossed a couple of political hot-potato cases in my lap, part of me was angry and part of me was proud. These were high-profile assignments in which a person could make some powerful enemies but also prove her skills. One case involved an arson fire that had been set by firefighters.

In March 1980, during a six-day strike by members of Local 42 of the International Association of Firefighters, some union members

16

set fire to a city-owned field near one of the Metropolitan Police stations. At the time of the strike, police officers were providing fire protection for the city. I was given the job of prosecuting some of the firefighters, and defending them was Larry Gepford, the former prosecutor. This was a felony case that was tried before Richard Sprinkle, who was probably the most respected judge in the courthouse. He and Gepford had known each other for years. *Holy shit*, I thought, *how many different ways is this going to be hard?*

The union members had been caught in a van with sterno cans adjacent to the field. I presented the evidence cleanly, and it was persuasive. But I made a fatal mistake: I failed to file a motion preventing Gepford from mentioning that the firefighters would lose their pensions if they lost the case. After I finished the first half of my closing argument, it was Gepford's turn. He stood up and, gesturing to the many family members seated in the courtroom, he asked the jurors to think about those families and what would happen to them if the firefighters were convicted and lost their pension benefits. I shot out of my chair to object, and of course the judge sustained it and told the jurors they should disregard the remark. But it was too late; there was no way to un-ring the bell. There was no conviction, and I felt lower than a snake's belly.

But two good things emerged from my defeat. Before the verdict came in, Judge Sprinkle wrote a letter to my boss saying that he was writing as the jury was deliberating and wanted to let him know that I had done a very good job in the courtroom, regardless of the jury's decision. Then later, when I was seeking public office, I stood before members of the firefighters' union and asked for their support. One of the guys I had tried to put in jail spoke in my favor during the endorsement meeting, saying essentially, "We don't have to worry about her doing her job." Ever since then, the firefighters have been big supporters.

Albert Riederer may have thrown me some curveball cases, but he was very encouraging when I decided to run for the state house, and he turned out to be one of my biggest supporters. But it was my mother and father who were the most important sources of advice throughout my political career. While Mom had been unsuccessful in her run for the Missouri Legislature, she was still the best politician I knew and a natural campaigner. Dad at the time was struggling; he had lost his job in the insurance business and seemed unable to cope with life. We would later find out that a brain tumor was altering his ability to function. He and Mom moved in with me in a small rental house in Kansas City. I was taking care of them in their time of need, but they would be my rock-solid foundation as I moved from the fight in the courtroom to the brawl of politics.

CHAPTER TWO

Bill and Betty

I was born Claire Conner McCaskill on July 24, 1953, which, according to the Climate Center at the University of Missouri, was the driest year on record in the state. Average Missouri rainfall is about forty-two inches; that year it was twenty-five. The big Missouri drought of 1953 would play a role in the direction of my life. At the time, my dad and grandfather were managing a grain mill, McCaskill and Son, in the southern Missouri town of Houston. The mill turned out flour under brands like Gilt Edge and Purity. The drought had a drastic impact on the mill's operations, and my dad began to consider doing something else.

Dad's ancestors had helped settle Texas County, where Houston was the county seat. My father was named William Young McCaskill, the Young from his grandfather on his mother's side, John D. Young, a respected leader who was elected as a Republican to the state legislature. Dad's paternal grandfather, William "Jackson" McCaskill, had been the county sheriff, elected as a Democrat. Dad's father, Clarence M. McCaskill, was an accomplished businessman who had also held public office. Leaving Houston would mean abandoning the family feed mill business and the town where everyone knew him and he knew everyone.

Still, in 1956, when I was three years old, Dad enrolled in a Prudential Insurance training program. My parents were plotting a course that would take us first to Lebanon, a town where my mom had grown up, and eventually to Columbia. Cutting ties to Houston probably broke my grandfather's heart, and it represented a major risk for my dad.

My parents lived in two different worlds. There were obligations that each had to fulfill, but each heard different callings. My mother was expected to have children and raise a family. She had witnessed what happened to her mom, a single mother. At the same time Mom loved engaging in public life outside the home. My dad was expected to take up the mantle of his father and run the mill. But he had other goals and interests that beckoned him to a life beyond the small town of Houston. And I'm sure my mother was pushing him. My parents followed their dreams as best they could while successfully raising four children and following the social rules of their era. When they told us we were free to take risks and that we could strive to be anything we wanted, it almost seemed as if they were trying to convince themselves they too were free.

The McCaskill and Son flour mill was not the only small business that played a role in my childhood. Sixty miles to the northwest, in the small town of Lebanon, was a corner drug store right off the main street of Lebanon. My mom, Betty Anne Ward, spent a lot of time there as she was growing up. Mildred Ward, her mother, worked at the drug store part time. Many years later, when my dad was struggling to earn a living in the insurance business, our entire family would feast on the hamburgers and hand-mixed milkshakes sold at the busy lunch counter in Conner Drug.

My middle name, Conner, comes from the man who owned and operated that store, Thomas Austin Conner. Before the arrival of chain drugstores, small-town establishments like Conner Drug were part of a community's beating heart. There you could sit on a stool at the soda fountain and order a cherry phosphate for a dime. For workers and shoppers at the noon hour, there was a short-order lunch counter, and at night, after downtown had buttoned up, the drugstore's fluorescent lights showed customers there was still time to fill a prescription or buy cosmetics.

Thomas Conner and his wife, Elizabeth, had no children. He was my mom's uncle, and he filled the role of father figure for my mom and her brother. He had married Elizabeth Harlin, one of W. T. Harlin's two daughters. Mildred, W.T.'s other daughter, had married a man named Sam Ward, whom she met while attending college in Tennessee. After their wedding, Sam and Mildred Ward moved to California, where Sam had dreams of making his fortune in the real estate business. They had two children: a son, Sam Jr., and Betty Anne, my mother, who was born in La Crescenta, California, in 1928.

Many years later Betty Anne spoke frankly about her "different childhood." Because Sam Ward Sr. drank and gambled, her mother moved out when Betty was four years old. Mildred took Betty and Sam Jr. back to Missouri, where they moved in with Mildred's parents, W.T. and Florence Harlin. Betty went to the first six grades of school in West Plains. That's where her grandfather sparked her interest in politics.

Like the McCaskills, the Harlins had helped settle the Ozarks of southern Missouri, where the valleys had become fertile with the soil washed down from the hillsides. That they set out to build a home in the hardwood wilderness testifies to their confidence and capacity for hard work. The family had first settled around

Gainesville, in Ozark County, about as far south as you can get in Missouri before you're in Arkansas. "The Harlins were very active Republicans," my mother recalled. "My granddad's brother was the mayor of West Plains for thirty years, and they had no taxes. He ran the city on the income from the utilities. So I think these little tinges of conservatism in Claire come naturally. She's heard both sides all her life."

Mom's love of politics began with her grandfather, William Tandy "Tan" Harlin, who went into the banking business in West Plains with his brother, Jim, around the turn of the century. Many years later she would fondly remember accompanying her grandfather as he passed out campaign literature for Alf Landon, the Republican candidate for president, around the town square in West Plains. Jim Harlin served as mayor from 1914 to 1944. He was said to have a quick temper that often led to conflict. Tan Harlin, on the other hand, was more level-headed and would sometimes step in to prevent fights between Jim and angry citizens.

In the small town of West Plains where the Harlin name was so well known, it was difficult for Mildred Ward to return without a husband. "My mother had it hard," Betty Anne recalled. "First of all, in those days you didn't divorce. And they were fairly prominent. And to go back home after that big wedding she had there some years before and all. After granddad died, she decided she would have to find a way to make a living. We moved in with my aunt and uncle. We were like the family that came to dinner. But we stayed."

My grandmother Mildred went back to school and learned secretarial skills at a business college. For the next two decades she lived with her sister, Elizabeth, and brother-in-law, Tom, in a tiny house in Lebanon. She worked at a state employment office and raised two children as a single mother. Betty Anne did not call her mother's sister Aunt Elizabeth but rather "Beppy," and when my sisters and brother and I came along, she was "Beppy" to us too. To my mother and her brother, Tom and Elizabeth Conner were like parents. "We were their children and they were interested in us," my mother said. "And they were wonderful to us."

Of course all this happened before I was born, but I later discovered what an interesting woman Grandmother Ward was. My dad called her "Old Ironsides." She taught me how to drive a stick shift, and she emphasized how important it was that I had an independent mind and that following trends "was for the birds." She was bright and assertive and wasn't afraid to speak her mind. And she was funny. When I was older, I once asked her why she didn't remarry. She replied, "When you make as big a mistake as I did, you just don't give it a second try. And besides, I have a full and happy life without a man."

Both Grandmother Ward and Beppy had a huge influence on me. They were college-educated women from a small town, and both of them were very strong in different ways. Grandmother Ward saved her money to spend on us but also to travel. She wanted to see the world, and she saved for many years to go on a handful of trips to Europe. Between Grandmother Ward and my dad's mother, Mary McCaskill, there's no question who was the modern woman. I don't remember ever seeing Grandmother McCaskill in anything other than a dress nor having a conversation with her about anything. Visits to her house were about antiques and cooking. I always sensed an undercurrent of judgment from her, that she didn't consider my mom traditional enough.

When I was still a young girl, living in Lebanon, I realized what hard workers Grandmother Ward and Aunt Beppy were. They would stay up late at night preparing food to be sold at the lunch counter in Conner Drug the next day. Then Beppy would work all day at the drugstore, doing whatever needed to be done. After my grandmother had worked from eight to five all week, she would get up on Saturday and bake bread all day. Every Sunday she would play the organ at church and then come home to prepare a big dinner for us. Afterward, rather than put her feet up, she loaded all the bread she had baked into her car. The members of our church who were sick looked forward to my grandmother's car appearing in their driveway late on Sunday afternoon. They knew that Peg Ward was coming with a loaf of bread.

Beppy ran the front end of the drug store and the lunch counter and the employees. She was four-foot-something, an absolute task-master when it came to manners, Emily Post with an attitude. She would make us hold our utensils the right way and would correct our pronunciation. You never used the word *sweat*; it was *perspiration*; you didn't have a *belly*, but a *stomach*. Drilling us on etiquette and manners, she instilled in us that it didn't matter if you had a lot of money, you had to have manners and use good grammar and handle yourself in a way that showed you had good values. Looking back, I realize that she was using her strong personality and her stern demeanor to give us the tools that would lead to confidence and success.

My parents met at the University of Missouri in Columbia, where Dad was working on a degree in business. During World War II he had served with a U.S. Army artillery unit in Europe. "He was one of the ones who figured where to aim the big guns" was how my mom later described his service. "He had a Bronze Star, and I didn't know about that until after he died." He went to college on the GI Bill while she pursued a degree in political science. They became acquainted through Betty's brother, who was in Bill's fraternity, Kappa Alpha. "We were both Democrats and one of the things that attracted me to Bill was his respect for women," my mom said.

Twelve days after Harry Truman gave the commencement address at my parents' graduation from MU they were married at the First Christian Church in Lebanon, on June 21, 1950. The bride, the daughter of Mrs. Mildred Harlin Ward of Lebanon, was given in marriage by her uncle, Tom A. Conner. They honeymooned in Colorado and returned to Houston, where my father was expected to someday take over the family feed mill.

Politics helped bring my parents together, and it would be their full-time hobby for the rest of their lives. They served on political committees, sealed campaign literature in hundreds of thousands of envelopes, and went door-to-door canvassing. They never let up. "I just liked the excitement of it," my mom would later say. "We kept up with it, and it was a people business and I thought it was something very worthwhile. I believed in it the old-fashioned way, that it's public service, and people who are willing to put themselves out there to do this are helping the country as long as their motives stay pure."

Their devotion to civic life nurtured me and my life's work. I got into politics for basically the same reasons as they did.

The first campaign my parents participated in as a married couple was Democrat Stuart Symington's first run for the U.S. Senate from Missouri in 1952. "There were six people in Texas County in favor of Stuart Symington, and we were two of the six," Mom explained. "You can imagine with his patrician ways how he went over in the Ozarks. But we were very impressed by him and decided to support him." Symington won, his first of four terms in the U.S. Senate.

In addition to working at the mill and dabbling in politics, Dad was president of the Houston Chamber of Commerce. In 1955 he invited the world-renowned clown Emmett Kelly to Houston for its annual Old Settlers' Reunion. Kelly, who had grown up on a farm near Houston and left in 1919, took my dad up on the offer and made an appearance. They still hold the Emmett Kelly Festival in Houston the first weekend of May.

But Mom was chafing under the watchful eye of her mother-in-law, who lived right across the street. Grandmother McCaskill had some strong ideas about how her daughter-in-law should behave as a dutiful wife, but my mom didn't want her decisions second-guessed. The last straw was when her mother-in-law confronted her about the two empty liquor bottles she had found in my mother's trash cans.

Dad was worried about his ability to support a growing family with the feed mill and hated that his financial security was tied to the vagaries of the weather. So he decided to try his hand in the insurance business, and we moved to my mother's hometown, Lebanon. With no son willing to take over the mill, Clarence McCaskill, my grandfather, entered into a contract to sell it to another company a few years later. He died the following year, at the age of sixty-one. "The sale was terribly hard on his father, but Bill was determined to get into something that wasn't directly affected by the weather," my mom said. "I was sad in a way, but Bill was right in making the move because he was much happier in insurance."

By that time my parents had two children: Anne Harlin McCaskill, born in 1951, and me, in 1953. My sister, Lisa Young McCaskill and my brother, William Young McCaskill Jr., came along after we had moved to Lebanon. In the years that followed, while Dad struggled to sell insurance policies, my family often got its meals free of charge at Conner Drug. "If Uncle Tom didn't have that drugstore selling hamburgers, we probably wouldn't have made it," my mom remembered. "We had a lot of hamburgers in that drugstore." Many years later, when I was elected and sworn in as a member of the Missouri House, Great Uncle Tom Austin Conner served as my escort. And when I gave birth to my son we named him Austin.

I have wonderful memories of our time in Lebanon. We loved those hamburgers at the drugstore and never had a clue that we were eating there because we were short on money. My sister Anne and I were given a tandem bike for Christmas one year, and we rode it all over Lebanon almost daily, regardless of the weather. A bike ride down to Conner Drug, a hand-dipped milkshake made by Beppy, and hours sitting by the comic book rack in front of the drugstore reading the latest editions of *Richie Rich*, *Archie and Veronica*, and *Casper the Friendly Ghost* for free—well, it just didn't get any better than that.

My mother was smart and used every trick in the book to get

us to read. When we misbehaved, she would sternly pronounce our punishment, forbidding us from going to the library for a week. Of course her reverse psychology worked. A perfect summer afternoon in Lebanon was Anne and I getting on the bike together, riding down the alley eight or nine blocks to the small public library where we would fill the bike basket with stacks of books, and then racing home to lie on a blanket in the backyard to read until dark. I used to sneak a flashlight into my bed at night so I could read under the covers after lights-out. It wasn't until years later that I realized Mom and Dad knew exactly what I was up to and had allowed me to break the rules to support my reading.

While Dad worked hard making cold calls to sell life insurance to put food on our table, he kept his hand in civic activities and politics. He understood that working in the community would also help his insurance sales. He chaired Lebanon's United Way Fund Drive and served as the Laclede County Democratic chairman. On Halloween during the 1960 presidential campaign, when I was seven, my parents had us say "Trick or treat and vote for JFK." It was in Lebanon that Mom's name appeared on a ballot for the first time. She ran for school board, finishing fourth out of a field of five.

Jackson Days was an annual statewide gathering of Democrats, and I think I went to my first one when I was nine. I spent a lot of time as a child handing out political literature and going to stump speeches, which was the traditional way in those days of getting to know the candidates. Everyone would gather on the courthouse lawn, and all the candidates would speak and hand out free emery boards and fans on which their names were printed. My sisters and I always had fun running around picking up all the political memorabilia people had discarded. At a young age we had quite a collection.

But there were some dark events too. When John Kennedy was running for president and my dad was chairman of the Democratic committee in Lebanon, a rock was thrown through the window of the party headquarters. My parents were certainly not his only supporters, but they were very much in the minority in conservative Republican Laclede County thinking that this young Catholic was the right man to be president. They told us there were people who didn't know any better, that the religion Kennedy practiced should not be considered among his qualifications to be president. After President Kennedy was assassinated, a book came out that covered that terrible event and the days that followed, *Four Days: The Historical Record of the Death of President Kennedy*. The following Christmas, Dad gave a copy of the book to each of us with a personal inscription. The night Bobby Kennedy was killed Dad got us out of bed to make sure that we were aware of what was going on.

When I was in fourth grade we pulled up stakes again and moved to Columbia. After six years with Prudential, my dad was promoted to manager, which gave him a larger sales territory and some responsibility for training other agents. He had made a successful transition into the insurance business, but it wasn't long before a new challenge loomed before him. In 1969 a controversy raged within the Missouri Division of Insurance over extra fees that were being collected by the state insurance superintendent and the chief counsel. For insurance commission hearings they conducted, the superintendent would receive an extra $300 and the chief counsel $250; that was on top of their state salaries. "It is the considered judgment of the governor that this practice should be stopped," wrote Paul E. Williams, Governor Warren Hearnes's legal assistant, in a letter to the division's chief counsel. The controversy and the news stories forced the resignation of Robert Scharz, the state insurance superintendent, and on May 22, 1969, Governor Hearnes announced the appointment of William Y. McCaskill as the new head of the state Division of Insurance.

It was a bold move for my father. While Dad knew a lot about the business of selling insurance, the appointment extended his responsibilities into unfamiliar territory. Suddenly he was asked to give advice to the legislature on what kinds of insurance should be sold

in Missouri, to decide how medical insurance companies should be regulated, and to explain the division's budget and fight for it in the General Assembly. He had to hire and fire employees, and anyone who complained to the governor about a claim or a premium payment was directed to talk to my father. It was a high-pressure job, and he took a pay cut to accept it.

Dad found the agency in turmoil from the bad publicity. Talking with insurance companies and other regulators, he learned that Missouri had a reputation for being lax in enforcement. One of the first issues he dealt with concerned an investigator in Kansas City who had been using the state office for political activities. In a letter to the governor, Dad suggested he be moved, explaining, "An investigator is one of our most direct contacts with the public, and the image of the department will to a great extent be determined by their impression of the investigator." In the end Dad requested the man's resignation.

I have a reputation for being direct and to the point, a trait I got partly from my dad. For example, Dad suggested to Governor Hearnes that he be candid in discussing "no fault" automobile insurance when it first became an issue. If he said nothing, Dad told him, it would look like "we have our heads in the sand." When a man complained about the agency's response to a complaint, Dad shot back, "I would strongly recommend you to contact your state senator and state representative and make him aware of the fact we are inadequately staffed to give more prompt consideration to complaints of the nature of the one that you sent to us."

Despite budget shortages, Dad promised aggressive enforcement and protection for consumers. He also openly addressed how politics helped him get his job. Dad was qualified, of course, but Hearnes also knew him from his work in the governor's political campaigns. The point Dad made was that good government performance and good politics can go hand in hand and work to the public's benefit. In a speech to 450 members of the Missouri Independent Agents

Association, he said, "The time has long passed for us to continue a naive and deliberate evasion of political involvement." The agents gave him a standing ovation.

As for my mom, here's how she described her role in a Christmas letter sent to friends and family when we still lived in Lebanon: "Betty Anne is busy remembering the fundamentals of baby care and keeping everyone dressed and fed. She also operates a taxi when the weather's too bad for the three girls to ride their bikes to school. Girl Scouts, Brownies, junior choir, bowling, the library and on and on."

If mom felt constrained by her assignments, she never let on. She once told an interviewer that she loved her role as mother and housewife. But she was also the kind of woman who wanted it all. She didn't have much patience for women who used the excuse that they worked outside the home to turn her down when she called to seek volunteers for some project.

My younger sister, Lisa Finn, has talked about how mom got to know everyone she met: "It started when I was too young to remember, the penchant my mother had for making friends everywhere. It got to the point where we didn't want to run errands with her anymore. We would pull into a gas station, and all of us would slink down into our seats because we knew by the time we left, the gasoline attendant would know our whole life story, how long we lived in the neighborhood, all of our names, and what our talents were. And my mother would know the attendant's name, his wife's name, how many children they have, and what they excelled at. And God forbid if it was election season. My dad used to joke, 'It takes my wife five minutes to make a friend and me a lifetime to get rid of them.'"

Mom was the original multitasker. In addition to all the roles she handled at home, she sought political and government appointments and volunteered for civic assignments. Her liberal views found greater acceptance in Columbia and Boone County, where hippies, university professors, college students, and Dixiecrats formed the political dividing lines. Mom was the vice chair of the Boone County

Democratic Committee; Governor Hearnes appointed her to the Missouri Commission on the Status of Women; and she was elected secretary of the Democratic State Platform Committee.

"I consider myself a liberated woman," she told a Columbia newspaper reporter in 1972. "I have my family's support and encouragement to go ahead with new activities. Many women wonder how I find time to do all that I do, but I think any woman who is motivated enough can find time for everything."

If life in Lebanon was an introduction to politics, growing up in Columbia was where my interest developed and matured. It was the middle of my fourth-grade year when we moved from Lebanon to Columbia, where I attended Russell Boulevard School. My parents encouraged us to read the newspapers and stay up on current events. At the supper table every night we had active discussions about what was going on. You had to speak up, speak loudly and quickly to get your point across. "It wasn't just say your prayer and eat your meal," my mom said later. "It was say the prayer and then let's get at it, let's discuss whatever."

The biggest political step my mom took was in 1971 when she ran successfully for the Third Ward seat on the Columbia City Council. Mom had been making speeches in favor of the Equal Rights Amendment, and her place on the City Council gave her a bigger platform from which to share her views.

The night she was sworn in was so embarrassing. I was in high school then, sitting in the audience. My mom walked into the Council chambers carrying a paper bag. When she got to her desk she pulled an apron out of the bag and put it on. Then she took out a vase of flowers, which she put on the Council table, then a picture of her four children. At this point I was slumped down in my seat hoping no one knew I belonged to her. But Mom knew what she was doing. She was making a point in a visual way, in a way that others could relate to. She said later, "I just decided I would emphasize the fact that a woman was there. A woman made it."

While Mom's service on the City Council made me proud, it also made me nervous. I could see how bold she was. She got a lot of attention once, walking out of the Council chambers and into the hallway, seeking out the student journalists from the University of Missouri who covered Columbia like a blanket, and loudly announcing that business was being conducted behind closed doors that was not exempted from the open meeting laws. There was also the time she got so frustrated with "the good old boys," as she would call them, that she left the Council dais and moved to the back of the chamber, where she proceeded to heckle her colleagues for the remainder of the meeting. While I didn't realize it at the time, I was learning valuable political lessons about risk taking and communication. I watched my mother talk straight and take risks for the things she believed in. Those lessons stuck. I also saw her alienate her colleagues in making a point at their expense, and that stayed with me too.

CHAPTER THREE

A House Hazing

Armed with a law degree and experience as an assistant prosecutor, I was equipped to find an important niche in the Missouri
General Assembly. My service there as an intern eight years earlier
showed me how women could be sidelined. I wanted to avoid that.
Changes were needed in the criminal justice system, and I hoped my
credentials would get me to the place where I could carry them out.
I was thrilled with assignments to committees dealing with criminal
law, but a group of men, all of them also lawyers, met privately to
plot how they could torpedo my attempts to change the law. So nothing much had changed: inappropriate and sexist comments still were
as common as weeds in August. I vividly remember walking through
the cluster of lobbyists outside the doors to the state house chamber
and hearing low wolf whistles. It wasn't unusual for even my married

colleagues to sidle up to me and make suggestive comments. Such behavior made for some very difficult days for me personally in the state capitol. I was pretty good at putting on a strong face, but I really wanted people to like me. I spent more time behind closed doors in my office crying than people realized at the time.

My entrée to elective office came courtesy of a vacancy in the old 42nd State Legislative District in Kansas City. To run for that seat, I had moved from my small apartment into a rental house at 6733 Locust Street, with my struggling parents now my roommates. The district encompassed Kansas City's southwest corridor and was generally bordered by the state line on the west, 63rd Street on the north, Troost Avenue on the east, and 95th Street on the south. To this day I can take you around the borders of that district even though the lines have changed several times since. I remember it so well because I knocked on a mind-numbing number of doors. Looking back on it now, I realize I was very naïve. I didn't have much going for me in terms of organized support; I didn't have money or connections; I rented, was single, and didn't even own a pet for the obligatory "family" photo.

My door-knocking campaign began in January for the election being held on November 2, 1982. It was difficult because I was still working as a prosecutor during the day and sometimes late at night. I used my vacation time to make up for it. Once daylight savings time hit, I was able to knock on doors from about four-thirty in the afternoon until it got dark. A few days before the election, my campaign got a jolt of energy when the *Kansas City Star* endorsed me: "Rarely does a candidate inspire us to believe that change indeed can come to the stodgy Missouri General Assembly. Claire McCaskill, the Democratic candidate in this race, is one of the few who does."

I won that election during a time of dramatic political change in Missouri. Earlier that year, state Senator Harriett Woods, who represented the St. Louis County suburb of University City, stood the Missouri Democratic Party on its head. She wanted the Democratic nomination to run for the U.S. Senate against the Republican incumbent John Danforth. She was the first viable woman candidate to make that groundbreaking move, and her candidacy generated waves of excitement. But party insiders, including Senator Thomas Eagleton, wanted her to wait her turn. Instead they anointed a Jefferson City banker, Burleigh Arnold, who had never before held public office. Harriett decided to go it alone. "I'd made all those speeches to women's groups about taking risks," she said. "I just couldn't let everyone down."

Harriett won the primary by a two-to-one margin, defeating Arnold by 123,000 votes. Once considered a shoo-in, Danforth found himself in a race for his life. Harriett was the only Democratic woman running for the U.S. Senate that year, and in the final weeks polls showed it was a dead heat. But just as voters were making up their minds, she had to cancel television ads when her campaign ran out of money. Out of 1.5 million votes cast, Harriett lost to Danforth by fewer than 28,000. In the wreckage of that race was a lesson, and it led to the creation of Early Money Is Like Yeast (EMILY's List), a progressive women's campaign fund that in the future would help female candidates, including me.

In January 1983 I was one of 163 members sworn in to the Missouri House. The General Assembly enjoyed a comfortable Democratic majority in those days, and the lawmaking process crawled along at a predictable pace. Before the advent of term limits, incumbents seemed sure of returning to the state capital year after year. Off the beaten track, where no interstate highways reached it, Jefferson City squatted on the banks of the Missouri River. State government was its major industry, and there wasn't much else to do there.

"It wasn't quite as serious as it is now," said Harry Hill, who was then a state representative from Adair County in a rural area of northern Missouri. "There were parties and there was a freshman class picnic and an interns' picnic and a lot of social events. And there were days when there just wasn't much to do." Doug Harpool, a Democrat from Springfield who was elected to the house the same year as I was, said, "I felt like there were a few talented people who ran the place, and everyone else pretty much enjoyed themselves."

In those days the legislature met until April 30 during election years and June 15 the following year. The weekly schedule had lawmakers showing up on a Monday evening and adjourning before noon on Thursday. Floor debates and committee meetings took place during the day, and the nights were filled with receptions, dinners, and parties sponsored by special interest organizations. Lobbyists spent freely on drinks, dinners, trips, and tickets to sporting events. Some men in the senate and house had relationships with women whom they had helped place on the state payroll.

I took office with a class of many talented people. One would become a governor; there were several future judges, as well as men and women who would go on to become directors of state agencies or business executives. Among them was a handful of lawyers. "There was a large freshman class that year because of redistricting," recalled Vernon Scoville, a state representative from Kansas City who had also worked in the prosecuting attorney's office. "All of the young lawyers at that time were competitors because we all wanted to be noticed, we all wanted to be chairman, we all wanted to have great legislation."

How I was treated then had a lot to do with how I looked. Gracia Backer, a Democrat who represented a district just north of Jefferson City, remembered that when I arrived in the capitol I had a "flowing blonde mane of hair." Harry Hill said my blonde hair then had "an electrified look. It was curly and stuck out. Another one of her friends used to call her 'the beacon.' You could see her in the crowd." It took a while, but I would overcome the "ditzy blonde" stereotype as the only female lawyer, though not the only woman, in the state house.

Some women were not happy with the fact that more women had arrived on the scene. I encountered a significant "queen bee" syndrome—women who had been there for a long time and who were very well established. They *liked* the fact that there weren't a lot of other women, and they were not as open as I would have liked; I think they felt threatened or jealous. I had a professional degree that allowed me to work in law, an area that had been traditionally off-limits to women, and this made some of them uncomfortable.

I was lucky as a freshman lawmaker to get guidance from Representative Karen McCarthy and Representative Annette Morgan. Both were Democrats from Kansas City. Karen had won her house seat in 1976 and already chaired a committee. Annette had been in the legislature for two years before I got there. At twenty-nine, I was the youngest; Annette was forty-four and Karen thirty-five. Often the three of us would share a ride to Jefferson City, and I absorbed a lot of legislative intelligence, history, and gossip from them on those 125-mile commutes. They helped explain the rules—written and unwritten.

My legal background earned me assignments on the House Judiciary Committee and the Civil and Criminal Justice Committee. This put me in a good place to sponsor legislation and, more importantly, to help others with legislation dealing with crime and the criminal statutes. I wanted to institute a crime victim's "bill of rights." I was also concerned about how the state's corrections and probation system had become a revolving door for career criminals. Violent men sentenced to life would be freed after a few years, only to commit another violent act and wind up back in prison. One convicted rapist sentenced to ninety-nine years was freed after serving only thirteen, and within one year he had raped again. I was working on a bill requiring that a person convicted of a violent crime had to serve a mandatory percentage of his or her sentence before being eligible for parole. The more violent the crime, the higher the percentage. That bill earned me the nickname "Hang 'Em High Claire." There were some bills I would not support. I refused to sign on to the "Make My Day" bill, legislation that extended a self-defense claim to include defense of property, essentially allowing someone to shoot a person even if his or her personal safety was not at stake—the precursor to today's "Stand Your Ground" law.

Lawyers are supposed to have an advantage, since the business of legislating is writing and passing laws. But the opposition I faced was not actually in the open; all of the six male lawyers who were elected with me demonstrated a more subterranean skill. They formed a clique to which I was not invited. They called themselves "the Six-pack." When my bills came up for consideration the Six-pack gave them special scrutiny: more questions and comments, more objections and proposed amendments. Once when I moved in committee for approval of one of my bills relating to the exchange of information in arson cases between insurance companies and law enforcement, a motion was made to table it. This was highly unusual, and I was taken by surprise. As my mom would say, a motion to table was as rare as hen's teeth. I couldn't understand what was happening.

Doug Harpool, the attorney from Springfield, finally came to my office early one morning and said, "You need to know what is going on. They are plotting against you." He had first noticed their unified effort to use the Civil and Criminal Justice Committee we all served on to slow down my legislation that would have required longer sentences for violent offenders. At first he thought it reflected the attorneys' deep-seated philosophical positions, but then he suspected that there might be more to motivate them; that it had less to do with the bill itself than who was sponsoring it. "After a while, I began to sense that there was jealousy developing about Claire and her success," Harpool said later. "More than just lawyers, but mainly it was this lawyers group. I felt like some of them were intentionally ganging up on her to hold her back. She was a fighter, and I think sometimes they liked to make her fight."

I cried about this later, but at the time I didn't let anybody know how upset I was. When I look back on it now, I realize how silly and immature they seemed. But at the time it was hurtful. Still, I didn't let the Six-pack get in the way of what I was trying to do. To be successful as a legislator, you have to put in a lot of hard work. You have to know your subject matter and be skilled in communicating its importance. You also have to demonstrate energy and a passion to convince others of the value of your position.

Certainly I had to confront some powerful people. The most powerful in the Missouri House was Speaker Bob Griffin. A Democrat from Cameron in northwestern Missouri, Griffin was first elected in 1970 and would serve as speaker from 1981 to 1996, the longest term in the state's history. I refused Griffin's request to vote for Tony Ribaudo, a Democrat from St. Louis, for majority floor leader. I wouldn't support Ribaudo because the man had once lied to me about a political deal he had made. And I told Griffin, "You shouldn't trust him." After he became majority floor leader, Ribaudo turned on Griffin and tried to take him out as speaker. I had a great "I told you so" moment.

Griffin was a very strong and effective leader, and he did give some women the chance to have an impact and make changes and develop their political careers. But I had trouble with him. I was too independent for him, and I paid a price for that.

Partly because of my independence, I didn't get a chairmanship as early as other people in my class. Besides Griffin, I tangled with Representative Mark Youngdahl, a Democrat from St. Joseph who was chairman of the Judiciary Committee, where many of my bills landed. And I had a couple of very public knock-down-drag-outs with Richard Webster, the most powerful man in the state senate.

At first I thought my ideas for legislation were strong enough to stand on their own. Over time, though, I learned that to get ideas across the finish line you had to overcome obstacles, massage egos, persuade doubters, box shadows, and ultimately compromise. Youngdahl was convinced that my minimum sentencing bill was too harsh, and as chair of the Judiciary Committee he had power to block it. I spent hours in his office explaining the bill, not from the perspective of a prosecutor but from the perspective of a juror who spends hours deliberating on a sentence only to learn that the years of punishment decided by the jury were meaningless because of Missouri's parole policies. Youngdahl eventually came around after I agreed to a slight compromise in the language.

"In the Ozarks we would say that she gave back as good as she got it," Harpool said later. "They would come after her and she would stand up and give it right back. Youngdahl was one that she wouldn't back down [from]. Youngdahl hated the minimum sentencing bill. I think he was impressed that she ended up sitting down and talking with them and doing some compromising with them, and he decided she wasn't this strident, rigid advocate, that she had enough political sense to know that sometimes you have to deal, and he was impressed with that kind of thing. It seemed like every day there was a new reason why that bill was not going to get passed. She maneuvered around this one and then they'd put [up] an obstacle and she'd maneuver around that one."

There were ongoing sexual relationships among some members of the Missouri Legislature, often involving married people, between members and between members and staff. But the only man in Jefferson City I had a relationship with while I was a legislator was Harry Hill, a fellow legislator who was also single. We were the exception to the rule.

Harry grew up on a farm in northeastern Missouri, graduated from the University of Missouri, and became a reporter for the *Kansas City Star*. Working from the newspaper's Independence bureau, he had interviewed Bess Truman and helped cover Harry Truman's funeral. After leaving the *Star*, his interest in politics developed while working for Democrat George Lehr in his successful campaign for state auditor. Elected to the house in 1976, Harry often found himself in Bob Griffin's doghouse. "We just didn't see eye to eye philosophically, and I was too stubborn to cave in," Harry

said later. "He finally did give me a chairmanship, the 'esteemed' Elections Committee, but I lost that right away because of insubordination."

We would go on trips together. Sometimes on special occasions, like Thanksgiving, my family would host him. He liked the martinis Mom made. Once, on a journey of several days, we toured the northeast coast, staying at bed and breakfast lodges.

"When we would go to parties, she didn't drink a lot," Harry said later. "She liked to have good possession of her faculties because she liked to talk to people, and if you drank too much you would say something stupid, or not remember what was said or not be alert. Sometimes she would be the designated driver because she didn't drink very much."

People started rumors and spread rumors and made up stories. There were remarks made *to* me and *about* me, some of it privately and some heard by others. Harpool recalled, "These guys would always joke that Claire was sleeping with everybody. They had no basis for any of it. Any woman who was successful, they'd accuse of having slept with somebody."

Sometimes I ignored it, sometimes I responded, sometimes I cried, and sometimes I tried to turn it into a joke. I had to figure out how to remain friendly and collegial so I could be a successful legislator, but I also had to learn how to avoid being marginalized and treated like a sex object.

Term limits now prevent a legislator from holding a seat for more than eight years, but in those days there were men who had been in the Missouri House for ten, fifteen, twenty years. Many were from rural areas, and some were big-city labor types. They were the old guard, the "good old boys." "[Claire would] walk by on the floor and they'd say something to her, laughing at her or kidding her," recalled Harpool. "She used her waitress skills well with these guys." There *were* moments when I tried to have a sense of humor, but in the end I had to face their remarks head-on.

Once a group of legislators took a bus to a restaurant at Lake of the Ozarks for dinner and drinks. On the way back, I was teasing some of my fellow legislators about how I had outmaneuvered them on a piece of legislation they opposed. One of them, who was drunk, proceeded to begin referring to me by spelling out an extremely disgusting word, "CUNT," several times, loud enough for everyone, including me, to hear. Sitting next to me, Gracia Backer recalled the episode. "He was back behind us on the bus, and he spelled out that word and it bothered Claire visibly. And then he did it again, and I reached around the bus seat and I grabbed him and said, 'If you don't shut your mouth, I'm going to knock your head off.' And Carole Park, a state representative from Sugar Creek, was sitting next to him, and she said he better stop it or he was going to get punched." He did stop.

At that time Kit Bond, a Republican, was the governor. He had been elected the first time in 1972 but was ousted in a close general election in 1976 by a dark horse candidate, Democrat Joseph Teasdale, a former Jackson County prosecuting attorney. Bond made a comeback, beating Teasdale four years later. One of the first times I met him was at a reception he held for the legislature at the beginning of the legislative session in January 1983. It was held at the Governor's Mansion, and I was eager to make a good impression. There was a receiving line with the governor on one end, his wife at the time, Carolyn, on the other end, and many of the other statewide elected officials and legislative leaders in between.

Just ahead of me as I was going through the line was Representative Winnie Weber. Winnie was known for her bluntness, her love of parties and alcohol, and her ability to be "one of the boys." She was famous for showing up on the floor of the house during votes in her long fur coat and teasing the men about what she had on under it. She would throw parties in her capitol office, and the governor, in a spirit of bipartisan friendship, would sometimes show up. Winnie had a good heart, but she came to the legislature at a time when too many women wallowed in the sexist behavior of the place in an attempt to be relevant and effective.

As we were waiting in line, Winnie turned to me and loudly said, "You're so young and pretty, and we're going to teach you a few things around here." I laughed nervously. She was a heck of a lot more relaxed than I was. When she got to Bond's place in the line, she turned and pointed to me and said to him, "She may be young, but she hasn't got these." I cringed as Winnie proceeded to squeeze her arms against either side of her large breasts, shaking them proudly for the governor. Mortified, I politely reached out to shake Bond's hand. He leaned down and quietly made a comment in my ear that made it clear he was not offended. Many years later, after I was elected to the U.S. Senate, Bond and I would represent Missouri in Washington from different sides of the aisle. He had been the governor when I arrived in Jefferson City as a wide-eyed young woman just off my first election, and later it felt a little strange to be his peer.

Winnie's behavior wasn't as egregious as Griffin's when he was speaker. Once I had to ask him for help and advice on how to get my first bill out of committee. He was on the dais and laughingly said, "Well, did you bring your knee pads?" I knew he was joking; the problem was that he didn't realize it was an offensive joke. This was one example of the bad jokes that were told. And that was many times the essence of the problem: Men in Jefferson City did not understand or comprehend how offensive their humor could be.

I made a decision to laugh on the outside at all the sexual harassment, while on the inside I used those moments to amp up my determination and focus to succeed. To this day I'm not sure that was the right response. I had convinced myself that only power would allow me to overcome an environment where too many people refused to take women officeholders seriously. The problem was, I was offending the powerful.

My biggest public dispute was with Richard Webster, a Republican who was the most powerful man in the state senate. A portrait of Webster now hangs in the senate lounge in the state capitol in Jefferson City, and there's a building named after him on the campus of Missouri Southern State University in Joplin. "Senator Webster had respect that bordered on fear," a newspaper columnist once said. A lobbyist put it this way: "The legislature is a computer game, and Dick Webster wrote the program."

His power flowed not from his political party nor from the district that elected him. As a Republican, he was in the minority, and he represented Carthage, in the southwestern corner of the state. His outsized influence came from his longevity, his deep knowledge of all the political rules, and his willingness to be ruthless. As the senate's minority leader, Webster brought fellow Republicans together with a splintered group of Democrats to choose the senate's president pro tem. As a lawyer-legislator, he did not amass a fortune in financial terms, but he did collect a lot of political IOUs. And he began cashing them in when his son, William Webster, entered politics. Dick Webster wanted his son to be governor.

When I was elected to the state house in 1982, Dick Webster had already been a member of the state senate for two decades. He was first elected to the house in 1948, and in the 1950s he served as its speaker and ran unsuccessfully for lieutenant governor and attorney general. When his younger son, Bill, expressed an interest in politics, Dick channeled all his energy and resources into boosting his chances. He helped bankroll his son's campaigns for the state house in 1980 and 1982 and the attorney general's office in 1984. The money poured in from lobbyists who owed the senator, and the elder Webster's campaign committee transferred thousands more to the son's. Once Bill was elected attorney general, Dick ran interference for him in the legislature. As a member of the Senate Appropriations Committee, he made sure the attorney general's office got everything it needed and much more.

The state senate was less partisan then, and minority party members could have major roles. Dick Webster's full-time involvement and interest, and his ability to manipulate the levers of power, made him a force to be reckoned with. One element of his strength was his ability to make trouble. Individual senators could get their point across in only so many ways, but a single senator with the power of the filibuster could scuttle a bill sent over from the house. Once Dick Webster barred a financial institution's lobbyist from entering his office, and for five years that institution failed to pass a bill it wanted. When the institution hired a new lobbyist, the bill sailed through without a problem. Dick was not someone you wanted to cross. On his perch as a senate appropriator, his wallop was larger than most of his colleagues'.

Griffin appointed me vice chair of the House General Administration Appropriations Committee, which handled the budgets of statewide elected officeholders. The chairman was Representative Bob Holden, a Democrat from Springfield. Holden and I came to the house in the same class. During the 1986 legislative session, we concluded that the budget was giving the office of attorney general exorbitant amounts of money. We decided we would expose that huge increase in appropriations and try to stop it. So we did up charts and graphs and had a press conference, declaring, "This is nepotism. These budget increases are not warranted. This needs to stop. This is just about the senator protecting his son. This kind of power is not healthy for government." The uproar was fierce, immediate, and bipartisan: Democratic members of the senate were quoted in the paper the next day calling *us* "asinine."

The next morning, after we'd succeeded in cutting the budget of the attorney general, I was sitting at my desk. Dick Webster sent a runner to my office down in the bowels of the first floor of the capitol to tell me, "I've been sent by Senator Webster, and he just wants you to know that all your legislation is dead for the session." And it was. He killed everything that had my name on it. Worse, during later conference committee sessions a lot of the money we'd cut from the attorney general's budget was restored.

From that experience I learned to anticipate the consequences of my political actions. In the immediate aftermath, I was able to maneuver around the Webster obstacle by asking other people to sponsor amendments for me. I ended up getting some things done, but I didn't get them done in a way that helped me politically. Until then I had been building a political record. I had written and sponsored the Minimum Sentencing Act. I had also handled and strengthened the state's domestic violence laws by granting victims economic support so they could move away from the person assaulting them.

But the Webster backlash continued.

A few months later, when I was up for reelection in the house for the third time, Attorney General Bill Webster swooped into my district to campaign on behalf of my Republican opponent, Addie Winslow. This was unusual. Winslow had been active in Republican campaigns for twenty years and was the coordinator for the Reagan-Bush campaign in the Kansas City area in 1984. She was a good friend of Kathryn Tiemann, Bill Webster's mother-in-law, who lived in my district. So they were bringing in some big guns to shoot me down. I assumed that Bill was trying to take me out either because I had given him so much grief about his budget or because he wanted to short-circuit any plans I may have had to run against him.

As it happens, people had begun encouraging me to run for attorney general in the election that was two years down the road. While the young Webster was my age, he had been attorney general since 1984. I didn't make any commitments. Some people told me that taking on Webster would be rough, given the influence of his father, to which I would laughingly respond, "You just don't know my mother." So I wasn't discouraging the talk. Some high-ranking Democrats were weighing in on the conversation as well; Harriett Woods and Vince Schoemehl, the mayor of St. Louis, were among them. Schoemehl even sent his car to Jefferson City to pick me up, and I remember thinking, *Man, this is a big deal*. Off we went to St. Louis, where a young state representative was wined and dined in a fancy restaurant by the mayor of the city and the lieutenant governor of the state, who happened to also be the first woman ever elected to statewide office in Missouri. They tried very hard to persuade me to take on Bill Webster, but I didn't want to run a race that I didn't believe I could win, and I first had to win my third term in the state house.

Many Catholics lived in my district, and running for reelection always meant defending my pro-choice abortion position. Opponents threw it at me again and again, and public meetings were loud and boisterous. I was okay with that; I wanted my constituents to have a chance to say what they needed to say. In the Waldo area of Kansas City, where people read the paper every day, I was confident that as long as I could explain my votes, I would be fine.

It was around this time that I began having a recurring nightmare. I dreamed I was standing at my desk on the floor of the Missouri House, waiting to be sworn in. As I stood there in full view of my colleagues and the spectators in the gallery, someone tapped me on the shoulder and said in a loud voice, "Claire, what are you doing here? Don't you remember? You lost." I didn't tell anyone about the dream, but many nights it woke me in a cold sweat. And it pushed me into overdrive during that last house campaign. The weekend before Election Day, I was near exhaustion, running on pure adrenaline. I could not sit still. My dad told me to take the day off. "There's no point killing yourself," he said. "You're a two-term incumbent and heavily favored to win." "No," I replied, "I've got to go. What if I lost by one vote?" As it turned out, I overwhelmingly defeated Addie Winslow, 6,705 to 3,817, a margin of 64 to 36 percent.

In the fall of 1987 the *Kansas City Star Magazine* published a six-page profile of me under the headline "Blonde Ambition." The subtitle was "State Rep. Claire McCaskill is the kind of woman who knows exactly what she wants. Everything." Written by Joe Popper, the story recounted my upbringing and early political career, told in the words of my family and friends. I don't know why Popper singled me out, but it was very controversial among my colleagues because it was such a long article. My mom added more controversy when Popper interviewed her and she discussed the fact that I was for the death penalty and she was against it. One of my quotes that the article highlighted was this: "Yes, I love a good fight, and that will either help me or be my downfall as a legislator. I'm headstrong and a bit independent and the type of politician who will either go a long way or just crash and burn. We'll see."

I was starting to make some headway in my personal life as well. As a young assistant prosecutor, I had lived in a very small apartment just off the Country Club Plaza shopping district in Kansas City. I had so little money I could not afford the parking fees downtown, so I took the bus back and forth to work every day. I didn't really have any friends in Kansas City since I had just moved there right out of law school. I had gotten into the habit of stopping in a neighborhood bar, the Granfalloon, when I'd get off the bus after work. I usually stayed for just one beer and then walked the few blocks home. It was a friendly place with a number of "regulars," much like the bar on TV's *Cheers*. I became friends with one woman bartender and some of the regulars, including a nice guy named Jerry Schanzer. In 1983, during my first year in the legislature, Jerry said, "I have a guy I want you to go to lunch with." That guy became my first husband, David Exposito.

David had evidently seen me in the Granfalloon and had asked Jerry to fix us up on a date. He and his brother John owned three auto dealerships in the Kansas City area, and Jerry assured me he was a "great guy." So I went to lunch with David. My first impression was that he was a handsome guy, a very smart guy, and a guy who was down to earth. He was dressed impeccably; his tortoiseshell glasses were fashionably forward, his fingernails buffed. His grammar was not perfect, and though he was charismatic he was not college-educated. But I was drawn to his high intellect, his authenticity, and his confidence. And he was fun.

We began dating and had a million laughs. We went to nice places and spent a lot of time talking about our upbringing and about his first, failed marriage. Before long I met his three children, and within six months it became clear that our relationship was headed toward something serious. I was still dating Harry Hill in the fall of 1983, and it was time to make a decision.

David was successful, but not successful in the same way as many of the men who surrounded me: a self-made man with only a high school education. I was painfully aware of how important it was that I find a partner who was confident in himself and who celebrated my success, as opposed to being threatened or intimidated by my career choice. David was both confident and charismatic and appeared to celebrate my success. After dating for a few months, then dating exclusively for about six months, we got engaged in early 1984 and were married in May. My mother was not convinced David was the right guy for me; she was worried about his lack of a college education and had concerns about our compatibility. But I was headstrong, and I was certain.

The early years of our marriage were high-flying. The car dealership seemed to be doing well; we went on a honeymoon to Europe and joined a local tennis and racquet club, and we bought a bigger house. Occasionally I was troubled by David's drinking, but I was confident I could make the marriage work.

Even though he had made some passing comments about not wanting more children, after our first anniversary I started focusing on conceiving our first child. With my legislative schedule it was a little tricky; casting votes didn't always mesh well with ovulation, and I was shocked to discover you couldn't just get pregnant when you wanted to. With laser-like determination, I became a slave to my body's cycles, sometimes driving home from Jefferson City for just one evening if I thought the timing was right for conceiving. It took over a year, but finally, with some help from fertility drugs, I got the result I was looking for in December 1986.

I was ecstatic. David was also very excited. I loved being pregnant. I was never sick and had very little fatigue. The only dark cloud during the pregnancy was how clearly I could now see others' drinking. There is nothing like being stone sober to make you notice others drinking heavily, especially members of your family. I began to tense up when I observed my mother or my husband drinking too much. I became convinced that they both had a drinking problem. But I pushed those concerns to the back of my mind and focused on the joy of our first child.

My first pregnancy earned three columns in the *Kansas City Star*. "Veterans of the General Assembly believe this may mark the first time a member of the male-dominated legislature has been pregnant during her term of office," the newspaper announced. It was interesting hearing my colleagues on the subject: "Gosh, how much weight are you going to gain?" "Do you need to sit down?" "Now don't get too excited, Claire, it might hurt the baby." I have joked many times about being tempted to force some of my antiquated colleagues into midwife duty right on the state house floor.

It was when I was pregnant that I learned from David that the correct spelling of his Italian last name was Esposito rather than Exposito. His grandfather lived in a small rural Missouri town, Nevada, and was embarrassed when an unrelated gangster named Esposito out of Chicago was in the newspapers. He decided to change the spelling of his family's name so no one would think they were related. David asked if we could use the correct ancestral spelling for the names of our children, and I agreed. So our three children were named Esposito, while their dad's name remained Exposito.

Austin Christopher Esposito was born at seven o'clock on a Sunday morning, September 6, 1987, at St. Luke's Hospital, weighing eight pounds, seven ounces. He was quite the celebrity. My room was jammed with dozens of floral arrangements from my colleagues, lobbyists, and friends. Senator Eagleton sent us a silver infant cup engraved with the U.S. Senate seal, and John Britton, the lobbyist for Anheuser-Busch, sent a baseball autographed by the entire 1987 National League Champion Cardinal team.

When I resumed my duties in the state capitol, Austin came along. There is a procedure in the legislature when special guests are introduced to the chamber, and all business, no matter how important, is interrupted. "This is the most special guest I will ever have," I said, introducing Austin. "I told him he can be anything he wants in life except a Republican." All of my colleagues felt like he was their child too, and when he came to Jefferson City with me for the legislative session in January 1988, he had many "babysitters." David was a terrific father: hands-on, involved, and loving. As it turned out, he was a much better father than he was a husband.

During the legislative sessions the year after he was born, I brought Austin to the capitol almost every week. But I knew it was going to be impractical to continue. I didn't think it was healthy for him to miss that much time with his dad, or to miss that much time with me, when he was so young. Although I managed that first year or so, I knew that raising a small child away from home was going to be extremely difficult. I made up my mind that I was going to go home and run for Jackson County prosecuting attorney; my old boss, Albert Riederer, had told me he wasn't going to run again. So just as my legislative career was winding up, I began laying the groundwork for jumping into a crowded Democratic race for prosecutor.

In my last days in the state house, I had one last confrontation with the Websters. Dick Webster, the senate minority leader, called me a "whore" to one of my colleagues while standing on the floor of the senate. He and my colleague were discussing one of Webster's bills, which I had amended to remove a provision that would have given too much political power to Attorney General Bill Webster over the hiring of private lawyers for the state employees' retirement system. In reaction I decided to invoke a house mechanism that allows a member to speak out on a point of personal concern, usually an especially controversial or unusual issue. When a member stands up to speak on a "point of personal privilege," things get quiet and everyone pays attention. After I heard about what Webster had said, I took the floor.

I told my colleagues that a powerful senate leader had made "a cruel and baseless insult impugning my moral character." I didn't mention Webster by name, but people knew who I was talking about. "Although my first reaction was anger, upon reflection, I realize the issue is not one of gutter comments unbecoming to any individual, much less an elected official," I said in my floor speech. "Rather the issue is misuse of power." After I finished speaking most of my fellow Democrats and even some house Republicans gave me a standing ovation. Later I told the press that Dick Webster was the source of the slur. His comment about me was not the last time a Republican would make such a remark. But the next time it happened, it cost someone his job.

Later Bill Webster ran for governor and was considered the front-runner in his race against Democrat Lieutenant Governor Mel Carnahan. By then Webster had acquired a national reputation by arguing abortion and "right-to-die" cases before the U.S. Supreme Court. Then scandal swamped his office. Some of his private attorneys, the hiring of whom I had tried to block, were caught up in the corruption of a state workers' compensation program known as the Second Injury Fund, a fund they were supposed to be protecting. Lawyers Webster appointed to defend the fund were in fact looting it. All of this dirt was exposed in a knock-down, drag-out fight in the Republican primary in which Webster narrowly defeated my future U.S. Senate colleague Roy Blunt.

But Carnahan defeated Webster in the general election, 59 to 41 percent, and four other Democrats were swept into statewide office. Two of the lawyers who worked for Webster's attorney general's office went to federal prison for defrauding the state. Bill Webster pleaded guilty to unrelated federal charges of conspiracy and embezzlement and was sentenced to two years in federal prison. Once a rapidly rising star in Republican politics, William Webster became the highest-ranking Missouri official to be convicted of a federal crime.

I wouldn't have traded my six years in the Missouri General Assembly for anything. I learned *so* much—about compromise, about the process of government, about how to get something done within it, about how to make allies and how to lay the groundwork and reach out to the right groups. I learned a lot about campaigning too, because I always had an opponent.

But even more important, I realized that speaking truth to power can be survivable and even a lot of fun. While it was really hard and discouraging at times, I did distinguish myself by being willing to stand up to Bob Griffin, Dick and Bill Webster, Tony Ribaudo, and others. I went toe-to-toe with some senate bullies and lived to tell about it. I figured out that their tactic was to try to get their way by intimidating people, and if you stood up to them, they would back off. I found that if you are informed and work hard, you can earn credibility. I went from being the young blonde with all the hair to being someone whom the senior members approached when they had questions about criminal legislation.

At a political dinner recently, I saw one of the old-timers who once had great power as the budget chair. His daughter asked me to come to their table near the back of the room and say hello, which of course I did. He was gracious and later wrote me a very nice thank-you note. That note meant a lot to me; that a man who had great power and seniority over me as a young legislator was now sending me kind words of admiration represented the distance I had traveled politically. Even members of the Six-pack have come around, asking me for help in getting federal appointments. And I call all of them friends.

CHAPTER FOUR

Madame Prosecutor

By the time I left the Missouri Legislature, it was no secret that someday I hoped to be governor. I wasn't broadcasting it, but if someone asked me, I did not hide my interest in gaining a bigger perch. It's nothing to be coy about, and it amazes me that people who run for office try to disguise the fact that they have ambitions for a higher one down the road. Women are particularly bad at saying they want to move up.

I had seen enough during my four years as an assistant to know I wanted to be the top prosecutor. The job gave you the feeling that you really had a grip on what was going on in the community. You could see the good you were doing and measure progress in real terms. It went beyond a "Lock 'em up" mentality: I had ideas for new approaches to get at the causes of crime. Also, if I became county prosecutor, I could be in Kansas City full time for Austin and for the other children I wanted to have.

Jackson County was heavily Democratic, so the prosecutor's race would be decided in the August primary election of 1988. But as I prepared to file, I discovered the situation on the ground had changed. Albert Riederer, my former boss who had served two terms as county prosecutor, liked being prosecutor so much that he decided to run for a third term. If I really wanted the job, I was confronted with the prospect of challenging him. Albert and I shared many of the same friends and supporters; now they would have to choose sides. I faced a tremendous risk; challenging an incumbent is always a high-wire act, and you don't easily recover from a fall. But as I weighed my chances, I knew my years in the legislature had given me significant and positive name recognition in the community, and I was aware of enough of the shortcomings of the office under Albert to know that I could make a good argument that change was needed.

I was thirty-four years old when I took what was to be the biggest political risk I had ever taken until then. While it angered some, it forced others to make their own calculations. Like a chess match, one move in politics prompts a countermove. For an incumbent in a primary, one of the most effective strategies is a crowded field. I believe Albert went to work to find another candidate to run in that primary.

On the last day of filing, just hours before the deadline, a woman named Carol Coe unexpectedly filed for the county prosecutor nomination. What had started out as a race between Albert and me suddenly became a three-way contest, with Carol cast in the role of potential spoiler. A member of the Jackson County Legislature, Carol Coe was an African American whose presence on the ballot would erode the support I anticipated from Freedom, Inc., a very important and influential black political organization in Kansas City.

What had been an uphill battle against an incumbent now

became much more difficult. It became clear very quickly that the prospect of a three-way primary was eroding the confidence of my supporters. The pressure began building to get me to withdraw from the race.

So we had a meeting. Some of my supporters were there, and Albert's supporters were there, as well as some people who were friends with both of us. I said, "Okay, I'll withdraw, but I want your word that you won't run again next time and that you'll support me." I made him get into a room with witnesses, and he had to say in front of them that he wouldn't run again in 1992. We memorialized his agreement with a handshake. I had been a candidate for prosecutor for about two weeks, and I came away with the lesson that in politics you can't be content with merely looking down the road for potential potholes; you have to look around corners as well. During that episode I left my supporters in the lurch, abruptly pulling out after they had promised me their help. I should have alerted them early on that I might have to get out, giving them time to mend their relationships with Albert before I made my departure announcement.

For the moment it seemed as if my political clock had stopped running. I had made the decision to leave the legislature and there was no going back. I wanted to have more children, so with one eye on the political landscape and another on meaningful work, I looked to my experience as a courtroom lawyer and decided to go back to the law full time. Louis Accurso, the aggressive young lawyer I had mentored on my trial team in the prosecutor's office and whom I trusted and respected, approached me to be part of his new law firm. We joined forces in the offices of Accurso, Stein, McCaskill & Smith. I concentrated on discrimination cases in the areas of sex, age, race, and disabilities. I also worked on insurance defense involving fire and fraud.

Work at the law firm was fun, but it wasn't the public arena. I enjoyed the give-and-take of a courtroom; I didn't enjoy the pressure of making a payroll and running a small business, and the paperwork bogged me down. I missed politics. So while I continued to work in private practice, I ran for a part-time position on the Jackson County Legislature in 1990.

In Harry Truman's time, a three-member commission, called "the county court," governed Jackson County. Truman was a commissioner, or "judge," although the work was purely administrative. There was an eastern commissioner who represented the mostly rural area around Independence, a western commissioner who spoke for the urban area of Kansas City, and a presiding commissioner. In 1972 the county government was remodeled to give power to a nine-member legislature and an executive. The legislature has six members elected from districts and three chosen at large. When I ran for the at-large seat held by Carol Coe, some referred to it as a "grudge match." It was not. It was simply a countywide race I could win, putting me in a stronger position for my anticipated race for prosecutor in two years.

This was my first election experience in which my husband's business became a campaign issue. It would not be the last. I've since learned that if you're a woman seeking political office, extra special scrutiny is applied to your husband's business. If you're a male candidate, much less attention is paid to what your wife does for a living. Coe found something to talk about when my husband's car dealership went out of business. Property taxes were owed, and I explained that as the business was sold the taxes would be paid. My own taxes were paid in full, and the only thing she could dredge up was the closing of the dealership itself. Clearly she was desperate and not thinking too clearly about the ramifications of what she was doing. Her own tax problems became fair game in the press, which disclosed that Coe had faced liens on her house and IRS garnishment on her salary for past-due income taxes. Primary election day mercifully put an end to the war of words. In the three-way primary I received 41,518 votes to 19,381 for Coe and 17,481 for a third candidate.

As a member of the Jackson County Legislature, I introduced a resolution to lower the minimum age for jurors from twenty-one to eighteen. I supported a requirement that legislators complete a detailed financial disclosure report to list sources of income and potential conflicts of interest. I testified in Jefferson City in favor of a bill prohibiting men accused of raping their wives from using marriage as a defense. At the time Missouri was one of nine states that still had the marriage defense option in marital rape and sodomy cases. "It's embarrassing that we live in a state where it's okay to rape your wife," I said at the time.

It wasn't long before I found myself campaigning against my old boss, Albert Riederer, who, although he had taken the private non-reelection pledge, was making noises that he was going to run again. So I had to *really* go after him. He had given me his word, and I intended to make him live up to it. I began publicly criticizing him and the way he was handling an antidrug program in the prosecutor's office.

Voters in 1989 had approved a quarter-cent sales tax to pay for a beefed-up antidrug effort, including increased law enforcement, drug treatment programs, crime prevention, and education. As a member of the legislature, however, I found that $411,000 was spent on computers that had nothing to do with fighting drug abuse. One year after the antidrug tax had passed, only one crime prevention group had received money. There were problems with the way the tax was being administered, and Albert was in charge. From my seat on the county legislature I had the ability to comb through the budgets and the expenditures. It was the first but certainly not the last time that I realized the value of government auditors. The county auditors were constantly fielding my calls, and I wore a path on the floor to their offices. My criticism was pointed and grounded in the numbers. I began calling for changes, including taking much of the power to fund programs away from the prosecutor's office. My remarks prompted people to try to convince Albert that he should not run again. So *he* backed off this time.

By the time I was running for Jackson County prosecuting attorney, David and I had three children. Madeline Esposito had been born May 23, 1989, and Lillian on November 12, 1991. That meant that one of the issues I had to consider while running for the top law enforcement job in the county was how to cast myself as a tough, crime-fighting prosecutor while having three children under six. If I were running for that office today, I would highlight my family and children as a way of showing I'm a multidimensional woman. But back then, in 1992, campaigning to be the first female prosecutor, it was a tricky path to take. Since no woman had ever held the office, I believed I had to emphasize the fact that I could be tough and no-nonsense. I worried that if people saw I was a mother of three small children they would think I was not tough enough for the job. And honestly it worried me that people might characterize me as a "bad mother" for wanting such a demanding job while I had three little ones at home.

My most meaningful endorsement came from the Fraternal Order of Police. It was *very* important that the police were supporting me, because that told the community the police believed I was tough enough to do the job. In my paid advertising, we made a point of mentioning that I was the only candidate endorsed by them. "We had to portray the tough-assed Claire McCaskill, the woman who had prosecuted all these arson cases," recalled Steve Glorioso, a local political operative.

One of my campaign themes, of course, was the antidrug tax. Too much of the millions raised was being spent on office equipment and administrators. I promised to assign a full-time auditor to the program to make sure the money was going where it was needed most. In my campaigning I emphasized that while others seeking the office were also experienced trial lawyers and prosecutors, I was the only one who had balanced a budget as a member of the legislature.

My primary opponent was Michael Shaffer, another former assistant prosecutor. Shaffer came from a prominent political family

and spent about $75,000 on a series of television ads, including one that attacked me because my husband owned a vacant house that had been vandalized and was used by drug addicts. In another ad he said, "In this year of the woman, why does she want to be one of the boys?"

His campaign outspent mine $173,069 to $103,686. But I was very careful about how I spent my money. He had spent his so early that at the end of the race, right before voters made a decision, I had as much time on TV as he did. This save-for-the-end strategy is one I carried forward to this day. This was also the first of many races where I learned you don't have to have the most money; you just have to have enough.

Campaigning in Missouri at that time had its weird and anachronistic moments. Thomas J. Pendergast, the corrupt political boss who once controlled Jackson County, might have been dead and gone, but some of his ways had survived. There was an old Jackson County political operative who would try to put a twenty-dollar bill in my hand every time I shook his. "Are you crazy?" I'd tell him, of course refusing the money. The fact that he felt comfortable offering it told me how many other politicians in Jackson County over the years had pocketed the cash.

Then there was the time I made a public campaign appearance in a hall packed with fire union members in Independence, and the leaders asked me if I could guarantee that in the event any member of their family got into trouble, I would "take care of it." At first I tried to deflect the question; I laughed, hoping the question was a joke, and responded that my office was not in charge of traffic tickets. No, the man insisted, they wanted to be protected in case of felonies! I was astonished at the request. "No," I responded. "If that's a requirement, I'm not your candidate." The man said he was asking the question just to see how I would respond. I defeated Shaffer 59,094 to 29,384.

When I became prosecutor, I was determined that instead of

thinking defensively, dealing with crime after it happens, we should think offensively and short-circuit the causes of crime. Our approach should be similar to community policing, a throwback to the old days of cops walking the beats. I convinced the judges, the police, and the defense attorneys that we would be more effective in fighting crime if we allowed nonviolent offenders who were in trouble because of their drug use to enter a program where they would be monitored by a judge, required to work or go to school, and required to receive treatment. I got pushback at first, especially from the police, but over time they came around.

The program was and remains to this day highly successful. I was one of the founders of the national drug court movement and have watched it grow to be an integral part of our criminal justice system. There are dozens of drug courts across Missouri, and thousands more across our nation. It is a cost-effective program that has a very low rate of recidivism. Every drug court "graduation" brought tears to my eyes as former drug addicts stood proudly with their formerly estranged family members cheering wildly. The day I saw members of the Kansas City Police Street Narcotics Unit standing and applauding the graduates was the day I knew we had accomplished something special.

We established the first domestic violence unit in the police department and in my office. We launched the Fathering Project, where we began bringing in dads who were not paying child support. But instead of threatening them with jail time, we carried out a program similar to the drug court, requiring them to participate as a parent on the theory that a father who is spending time with his child will be more inclined to pay support. This approach was developed after asking a simple question: If what we're doing now is not working, what should we do instead?

We did a sting operation to intercept methamphetamine precursors. After concluding that people hooked on meth and dealing drugs were not deterred by criminal prosecution, we went after the retailers who were selling the ingredients in bulk to make meth, and we began making real progress.

When most politicians talk about crime, they make it a simple issue of building more prisons and locking people up forever. But fighting crime is much more complicated. You've got to be in the schools, you've got to have treatment centers, you've got to be in juvenile court. A part of me still misses the job. We had the largest prosecutor's office and handled more felonies than any other office in Missouri.

If you're in public office there is a tendency after a while to start thinking of yourself as a big deal. But children have a way of keeping you grounded. I certainly learned not to take myself too seriously when my son, Austin, who was in second grade, announced, "Mom, I've got to write something about what you do during the day." I sat down with him, and while I didn't say my office handled between eight thousand and ten thousand felonies a year and that I had a staff of hundreds of lawyers working for me on the most serious crimes imaginable, I did tell him, "Honey, I am the most important prosecutor in Jackson County. I'm the boss. I'm in charge of all prosecutions. I'm the one in charge of putting all criminals in jail. I'm a big deal. I'm *the* prosecutor."

I expected that he would write one of those heartwarming essays you can put in the scrapbook and read over and over again. But about a week later I received an envelope from Austin's teacher. It was sealed, which is always a bad sign. Inside was a brief note from the teacher, saying, "I thought you might like this for your scrapbook." It was paper-clipped to Austin's red Big Chief tablet paper, on which he had written the headline "What My Mom Does during the Day." The first line said exactly this: "My mom is the best prostitute in Jackson County."

That's what you get for taking yourself too seriously.

Unfortunately being county prosecutor has also left me with mental images I can never forget, of crime scenes I encountered.

The job brought me face-to-face with behavior that we all like to believe is not possible from human beings. The children's cases were the hardest.

One case in particular I still dwell on. William Burst sexually assaulted, then suffocated a six-year-old girl, Natasha Lawson, and then murdered her mother, twenty-five-year-old Tonya Matthews. Burst admitted that he suffocated the child; hours later he hacked Matthews two dozen times with a hatchet. That was one of the cases where I asked a jury to put someone to death. I personally prosecuted Burst, and at his trial I used my closing argument before the jury to demonstrate how long it took for the little girl to suffocate. The medical expert said the child would have stopped struggling after one minute and that it would have taken a full three minutes to suffocate her. I stood silently before the jury for three minutes to demonstrate how much time Burst had had to think about what he was doing. After the jury deadlocked on whether he should receive the death penalty, the judge sentenced him to life imprisonment without parole.

I spent a lot of time with the victims' families and with the victims themselves. I witnessed brave victims of rape using the most difficult, painful, and private moments of their life to seek justice. I've also witnessed victims standing up and having the cathartic experience of talking about what they think should be done to the person who did them harm. That hadn't been possible before we worked on the Victim's Bill of Rights in the legislature.

Missouri has 114 counties plus the City of St. Louis. Each has its own prosecutor, whose job it is to follow an investigation to its end, pursue redress or punishment for a crime, and institute criminal proceedings in behalf of the state. The state attorney general has virtually no authority in this area. Lawyers who work for the attorney general handle appeals of criminal cases and may come in to help out local prosecutors, if asked.

In 1992 Democrat Jay Nixon was elected Missouri attorney general in the wake of the Second Injury Fund scandal that so damaged Bill Webster's reputation. Nixon realized that making the attorney general's office a law enforcement office was good politics. There was one problem, and that was that the attorney general in Missouri has no jurisdiction over criminal cases. In Missouri local prosecutors handle all state crime, with the attorney general doing only the appeals.

Until Nixon, the attorney general's office got appointed to handle criminal cases in the unusual instance when a local prosecutor had a conflict. But he busied himself with hiring special assistant attorneys and offering their service to part-time rural prosecutors. He took advantage of the fact that many of the part-time prosecutors who are elected in small counties typically don't have the experience or the resources to handle a complicated homicide case. That's how he got his foot in the door of directly handling criminal cases. Those of us who were full-time prosecutors were not willing to let him open the door any further.

On February 28, 1995, Nixon sent me a nineteen-page letter informing me that his office had uncovered evidence indicating that House Speaker Bob Griffin had violated gaming statutes. The allegations focused on what Griffin had done on behalf of gaming companies that were seeking licenses to open river-based casinos in Missouri. The attorney general said his office was ready to prosecute these offenses if I would just step aside. He had hired a former assistant U.S. attorney now practicing law in St. Louis to help prepare the case. Nixon wanted me out of the case, insisting that I had a conflict because I had served with Griffin in the legislature. The fact that he wanted to benefit from the publicity that would accompany this case became obvious when the letter was leaked to the press.

Nixon's claims against Griffin prompted the three local prosecutors with jurisdiction over the case to confer about his effort to take it from them. In Missouri gaming licenses are controlled by an agency based in St. Louis County, so the county's prosecuting attorney, Bob McCulloch, was involved. Since Griffin did his work as speaker in the state capital of Jefferson City, Cole County's prosecutor Richard Callahan weighed in. And since Nixon sent the case to me to start with because Griffin's law firm was based in Kansas City, I was involved as well. So the three of us jointly examined the allegations based on the evidence Nixon had accumulated. There wasn't much there.

It became clear how little evidence there was against Griffin when the three of us traveled to Nixon's office in Jefferson City to discuss the case with him and his special prosecutor. We asked the special prosecutor how he would get the needed evidence. "That's simple," he replied. "I'll call that witness in front of the grand jury and compel his testimony by giving him immunity." There was dead silence in the room. Finally McCulloch looked up and said, "That's going to be hard in Missouri because we don't have witness immunity."

After reviewing the materials Nixon's office had given us, the three of us issued a joint statement saying that Griffin had broken no state laws. Our statement turned out to be correct. Two years later, when the U.S. attorney's office in Kansas City filed charges against Griffin, none of them had anything to do with the allegations that Nixon had made or the issues that we investigated. Griffin ended up pleading guilty to charges that he accepted a $5,000 bribe from a political consultant in exchange for his influence to get her a lucrative lobbying assignment from road contractors. He was sentenced to four years in federal prison.

As a prosecuting attorney and an officer of the Missouri Prosecuting Attorneys Association, I also served on the board of the National District Attorneys Association. This role enabled me to contribute to the discussion about fighting crime on a national level. For example, when Attorney General Janet Reno wanted to explain President Bill Clinton's anticrime package, she met with the board of our organization.

Although I welcomed board membership and all that went with it, it sometimes took me out of town. That was the reason I was in Orange County, California, on one of the worst days of my political career.

Ironically enough, it was my forty-first birthday, July 24, 1994. That evening I got an urgent message to call my sister in Kansas City. When I got Lisa on the phone she said that the ten o'clock news had just reported that David Exposito, my husband, had been arrested for smoking marijuana on a gambling boat in Kansas City. My first reaction was that it had been a mistake, that it was not my husband but his son, who was also named David, who had been arrested. Because I was the prosecutor and obviously wanted to avoid any appearance of trying to influence the case, I did not call the police. But I did reach out to my husband's friends. That's when the reality began to sink in. It *was* David, my husband. He had done an idiotic and destructive thing while I was half a continent away.

Eric Criss, the Missouri State Highway Patrol trooper assigned to the Argosy riverboat casino, had noticed David standing on an outside deck. Walking out the door, the officer smelled what he thought was marijuana and saw a half-smoked marijuana cigarette on the deck directly below. He ordered a security officer to retrieve it, and when he searched David he found a black plastic container with about four grams of marijuana. A municipal court date was set, and my fifty-three-year-old husband was released after posting a $212 bond.

When I became prosecuting attorney, I knew there were a lot of benefits associated with the job. I was treated with respect in a whole lot of places. I also knew when I ran for that office that my personal life was fair game. The fact that David and I were man and wife had once elevated to news-story status developments related to his business, and just a year earlier our names were in the paper in a lawsuit over business loans for David's failed car dealership.

I booked a flight for the next day, tossed and turned during a very sleepless night, and the next morning was on the telephone dealing long-distance with the chaos that was happening at my home. The media had camped in the front yard. Reporters even approached my babysitter, asking, "Where is she? When will she be back?" The situation was bad enough without the media invading our private space; even worse was that reporters believed I was hiding out.

I was getting a lot of advice on how to handle what had happened. People told me, "You need to come back and say he's innocent until proven guilty" and "You need to have a press conference and hold hands and say he's going to seek treatment." I decided that I was going to say exactly what I felt: I was mad as hell—mad that he'd been such a jerk and had done something so stupid. When I returned I immediately faced the press and public. On a previously scheduled radio appearance, I said, "You know, it's going to take about a month before I can resist the urge to kill him."

I then held a news conference and said, "Spouses deceive spouses with some frequency in our society, but most of the time it doesn't carry the pain of becoming public. I'm embarrassed, I'm mad as hell and I'm disappointed." I said I was aware that before I was married to David, he smoked marijuana and that I believed he had stopped. After the riverboat incident, I questioned him again and learned otherwise. "He has told me that on very rare occasions out of our ten-year marriage, he has smoked pot, but only away from our house and only when I was out of town. I have never seen any illegal drugs in our home, and he has assured me at no time were there any in our home." Asked about punishment, I replied, "The judge is going to be a lot easier on my husband than I will be."

My remarks touched a nerve. People sent me notes saying, "Hang in there." Someone sent me a prayer written on a piece of paper, and another sent a "Thinking of you" card attached to a bouquet. Many of the letters of support were from strangers, most of them women. One said, "I want to congratulate you on an uncanny ability to deal with adversity." A bunch of yellow roses included a card: "Tough times don't last. Tough people do."

People are very forgiving of human frailties. They are unforgiving of people who aren't willing to take responsibility for their mistakes or who aren't willing to be truthful about it. Harry Truman's career taught me that being up front and saying exactly what you think is usually not going to get you into trouble.

David pleaded guilty to marijuana possession and was sentenced to a year of probation plus twenty hours of community service. The Riverside prosecuting attorney said the sentence was similar to that given to others with the same charge and no record.

To this day it is difficult for me to talk about the end of my first marriage. I'm not good at failure, especially when it causes so much pain to people I love. David was raised in a household where there was not a lot of outward affection. He told me he didn't remember his parents hugging and kissing. It was quite an adjustment for him to find himself in the McCaskill clan, where everyone is very affectionate, always telling each other how wonderful they are. My parents used positive reinforcement constantly; David said his parents were constantly warning him he would be a bum. Those differences caused cracks in our relationship. I needed positive attention, and David chafed under the requirement to show some. I would push him to be more outwardly supportive, and he would resist. That usually resulted in his withdrawing. The more he withdrew, the more I threw myself into my work, almost as a passive punishment of him. It became common for him to give me the silent treatment and for me to use the excuse of work to be unavailable.

The bright spot in our sometimes difficult relationship was our children. I can't overstate what a loving and present father David was. With the birth of Austin, I saw a man who could show affection easily toward his son. He threw himself into parenting, insisting on handling more than his share of bath time, feeding, and diaper changing. When Maddie was born two years later he once again showed his character and his love by thinking of our children before himself. And we had wonderful fun together. Every weekend we would plan a family outing, and if a crime was committed that required my presence as prosecutor, he would go right ahead and take the children on our planned activity without me. David was a great father, and that helped paper over some of the serious cracks in our relationship.

But when his withdrawal became more regular, it made our marriage more difficult. I too must shoulder some responsibility, of course; I was too consumed with three small children and a very big job to put much work into the relationship. In the end I believe the most difficult times in our marriage had three major causes: the failure of his business, the continuing success in my career and my focus on it, and alcohol.

David and his brother, John, had great success against long odds. They began working as young teenagers wholesaling cars and acquiring real estate. They developed a solid reputation as hardworking "car men" and enjoyed respect among their business peers at a young age. They scraped and pushed and took risks in acquiring new car dealerships, first Chevrolet and then Pontiac and BMW.

When I met David it appeared to me, and to the world, that their business was successful and strong. It turns out they had always been undercapitalized. They never had the equity or the credit to fully succeed in the volatile world of new car sales. And they began to argue with each other as the pressure mounted. I became the go-between, and when it became obvious that the dealerships would need to be sold, I ended up in the boardroom of the bank trying to do the workout. At that point, in the early 1990s, David's relationship with his brother was poor and we were struggling. The more he needed my help, the more he resented me.

The dealerships were sold, and David, as a resourceful businessman, turned to some of his real estate for his next enterprise.

He developed a golf driving range on some of the land that he and John owned. I was proud of his work ethic and his determination, and I was supportive of his new endeavor. But I'm convinced that he was bitter and hurt over the failure of the dealerships, and that fueled the other big problem in our marriage: his drinking. We had partied before and during the early years of our marriage, but with the demands of my career and the children, I cut way back. I still had a glass of wine when we went out to dinner, and an occasional margarita, but hard drinking was over for me. Not for David. Near the end of our marriage, he finally acknowledged that he was an alcoholic. It was a demon he never completely conquered.

In May 1995, just after our eleventh anniversary, I told him I wanted a divorce. I already had the paperwork done, and, after a brief but harmless outburst of anger, David accepted that our marriage was over. He signed the divorce papers without even reading them. He trusted me; he knew I would never do anything to hurt him or his relationship with our children. David and I both understood that the most important job we had during the divorce, and after, was being good parents. I worked hard at making sure he had lots of quality time with the children, even after we moved to Jefferson City. My children have never heard an ugly or negative word from me about their father, nor from David about me. My children remember him taking them out to the driving range to put up yard signs for my elections after our divorce. David was a special and unique man whom I cared for deeply and my children loved desperately. That is why when his death came, ten years after our divorce, it was so difficult for all of us.

CHAPTER FIVE

A Statewide Office

A fter my divorce my focus was on my children and my work. There was no time for anything else. My children were seven, six, and three when David and I parted in 1995. I was the elected prosecutor in Kansas City. As a single mom with a demanding job, I learned quickly that there would be little if any personal time. I hunkered down, trying to be the best mother possible and continuing to eye the future for political advancement. My mother and my sister Lisa, who were both in Kansas City, were there for me and my children. My brother, Will, and my sister Anne provided great emotional support. I may have been a single mom, but I was held up by a bedrock foundation of family encouragement.

I vividly remember talking with a victim of domestic violence in the months after my divorce. She needed housing near a bus line because she was working three jobs to support her two small children, and she was worried about paying the electric bill for her one-bedroom apartment. As I drove home from work that day, I vowed to never again complain about the pressures of being a single mom.

But being a single mom was lonely. I missed the companionship of another adult, especially on the weekends that the kids were with David. But dating? I just couldn't see it. Certainly the bar scene was out of the question, and I politely declined when acquaintances wanted to "fix me up." Part of my reluctance was rooted in the belief that most men would be put off by my career and the public role it entailed. The end of my marriage was colored by my belief that my success had been part of the problem. I felt burned and hurt. And at that point I wasn't sure in which direction my career was going.

Luck, timing, and opportunity all play a role in politics, and they sometimes seemed like three offensive linemen opening up a hole just for me.

In the fall of 1997 Auditor Margaret Kelly announced her retirement. A few months later, Governor Mel Carnahan's office called and asked if I would join the governor for lunch in Kansas City in a few days. Of course I said yes, curious about the reason for the invitation. We were meeting at the Kansas City Club downtown, and as I entered the dining room I saw the governor sitting by himself in the corner waiting for me. I noticed his security detail nearby, but not within earshot. As we ate he began a hard pitch for me to run for state auditor.

I quickly said no. I explained that I had my dream job, that being a prosecutor allowed me to get in the courtroom and have a real impact on public policy through the outreach of my office. The governor, a Democrat, kept talking: "We have won every statewide office except auditor, and, Claire, I'm just determined that we win that office." Again I rejected the idea, but he refused to give up. "You can shape the office, go after waste and fraud wherever you want. You have serious power in that office to make government work better and gain an important profile when it comes to the financial matters of government." I again replied, "No, I have three small children and I'm divorced. I think a statewide run as a single mom is too tough. And then, if I win, moving my children to Jefferson City, where I won't have the support system of my mother and sister, is a nonstarter. No."

It was clear to me that he was not giving up. His parting words were "Remember, both Governor Kit Bond and Governor John Ashcroft were state auditors." Those words kept popping into my brain over the weeks that followed as I began to consider an option that was high risk and unthinkable when first proposed.

The auditor is the state's financial watchdog. The agency can drill down into all levels of government—state, county, and municipal—to make sure the taxpayers' money is being handled responsibly. The auditor doesn't have to wait for the police to bring a case; I could go ahead if I thought funds were being misused or expose that there was no case to be made. I saw similarities between auditor and prosecutor; for one thing, both perform investigations. The auditor's may be a financial investigation or a performance investigation, but still you must have all your facts. You have to make *sure* you're right. And you have to be able to present a case in a way that people understand. That's not much different from what a prosecutor does when he or she files a case. It began to seem like a wonderful opportunity to have a positive impact.

Another attractive asset was how that office pops up in the election cycle. While every other statewide constitutional office is elected during the same years as the president, the auditor runs two years later. The timing really sets the auditor apart and makes it a little bit easier in terms of getting the attention you need to become electable. The auditor serves a four-year term, so you are in a position to run for another statewide office in the interim. And if you lose, you still have the auditor's job.

But in addition to family considerations, the three letters "CPA" held me back. Since 1974 every state auditor had been a certified public accountant; it had become almost a tradition. If I were to win, I needed to convince people the job was not about being a CPA; it was about having knowledge of state government, knowing what to audit, and prioritizing resources.

I sought counsel from my mom. She and Dad had moved to Kansas City in 1980, and Dad had passed away in 1993. Mom struggled afterward, and I continued to worry about her drinking. But she had finely tuned political instincts and was still my go-to for career advice. Her opinion of my run for state auditor? "Go for it, and I will help you." It was not the first time, nor the last, that my mother gave her seal of approval to my ambition and my risk taking.

The election was in November 1998, and I began in earnest to run at the beginning of that year. With only six months to raise over a million dollars, I had to sprint. Two others who sought the job were CPAs, and I was really running against those three letters. My argument was this: "Initials behind your name do not make you a leader. What makes you a leader is the willingness to shake things up. State law does not require the auditor to be a CPA. I can hire a lot of good CPAs. And we will be expanding the responsibilities of the auditor's office."

We ran that campaign on a shoestring. There was no extra staff to ferry me around, so I would load all three of my children into the car near their bedtime to drive across the state. They would sleep, and I would drive, arriving in Columbia or Springfield or St. Louis late at night. At their ages, it made the car trips much less eventful, since I wasn't refereeing disagreements or answering "Are we there yet?" I would sleep-walk them into a motel room we would share for the night, many times all four of us in the bed together. We would then be ready to campaign together early the next morning.

They were ten, nine, and six as we crisscrossed the state that year. I was lucky that many of my supporters and volunteers would help entertain my kids while I gave a speech or worked the room.

One of my favorite stories from that year of campaigning came from Jack Hackley, a longtime friend and supporter who was entertaining Austin while I was giving a speech. Austin was in love with motorcycles. He talked about them constantly. I had told him repeatedly that motorcycles were too dangerous, that he could not have a motorcycle ever, that it would only happen over my dead and lifeless body. When Jack and Austin were walking around they saw a motorcycle. Jack lifted him up to sit on it and asked him if he would like one. Austin promptly replied, "Yes, I'm getting one the day after Mom dies."

I knew how to run this campaign. Once again I saved my money. We had a little hovel of an office in a basement without a window. I had two on my staff. There were no bumper stickers, no buttons, no yard signs, no entourage. We saved everything for television.

Every day my heart was beating faster because I could see, I could *feel* my opponent, Chuck Pierce, coming. I could see we were buying about the same number of ads. Pierce was the deputy state auditor, and he had an ad graphically showing all the audits he had done, piles of paper stacked high, and then it showed that my pile had nothing. It was pretty effective.

In the end I think Jim Nutter was one of the main reasons I won. If the Republicans had given more money to Pierce earlier, they could have beaten me easily. But Nutter came to my rescue, and I didn't even know it was happening until it was almost over.

I was at my son's football game at Visitation Catholic School when a cameraman showed up and began filming me. It was weird. I had another mother ask him what he was doing, but he wouldn't answer her. A week later I got a call from Bill McKenna, my former legislative colleague in St. Louis, who said, "That ad of yours with you at your son's football game is unbelievable, it's so good." I had no idea what he was talking about. It turned out that Jim Nutter had hired the cameraman and somebody to produce the ad and had spent $40,000 on cable television in St. Louis County. That ad ran for four or five days at the end of the campaign, and I had no idea until later who was responsible for it.

James B. Nutter Sr. is a successful businessman from Kansas City who, over more than fifty years, built an empire in the private mortgage field. In childhood he became interested in politics, and as a college student during Truman's 1948 presidential campaign, he worked as a ward runner in Kansas City, tracking down voters and making sure they got to the polls. Over the years he had contributed a fortune to Democrats running for public office, including me. He never asks for anything. He's only interested in supporting good Democratic candidates. And he deeply believes in women holding office.

With the help of Jim Nutter's campaign commercials in the St. Louis area and the strong support of people in the Kansas City community, I was elected auditor. Jackson County, Clay County, Platte County, Cass County, and Lafayette County—the people in those areas felt they knew me due to my extensive exposure on both television and radio during my time as Jackson County prosecutor. Those three letters didn't count so much after all. I ended up with slightly more than 50 percent of the vote.

The voters had given me a big promotion. As auditor, I would be, as one newspaper reporter quipped, in a much better position to stick my neck out. Soon I was taking on state government's sacred cows and questioning the spending habits of state officials, judges, university presidents, and even a beloved college basketball coach. I would tangle with special interests in the drug industry, public education, and well-heeled financial investment firms. Pet owners would grow to love me for my audits of the "puppy mill" industry, while my name became mud with nursing home operators. Before my time as auditor was over, I would be compared with a prostitute, have an ex-convict for a Republican opponent, meet and marry a new husband, and in the end turn the Democratic Party upside down by challenging the incumbent governor.

All that lay in the future as I attended a going-away party in the prosecuting attorney's office, which I had directed for six years. My goal has always been to leave an office in better shape than it was when I entered it. I was proud of what we had achieved. In one fiscal year, Jackson County sent nearly one thousand offenders to prison, more than in any other Missouri county. Most were repeat offenders, violent people. The office's bad check unit had been expanded and automated; our recovery rate rose from about two hundred checks a month when I came in to more than two thousand when I left office. I tried to foster greater cooperation with the police, especially to deal more effectively with domestic violence cases. I also campaigned successfully for the renewal of the county's antidrug tax and helped overhaul the program. We created drug courts that were considered a national model. And my office achieved a 100 percent increase in prosecuting drug trafficking.

At the same time, I was able to put programs in place for which women were traditionally accused of being too soft, of being "just a social worker" or worrying about mothers and babies instead of worrying about locking up criminals. I managed to achieve a delicate balance of being tough but with a softer approach.

Our move to Jefferson City was hard on my children, who were reeling from the knowledge that they were being separated from their dad. Austin particularly had a very difficult time, and my guilt was significant. I found a house and enrolled my children in the local Catholic school. One of the luckiest discoveries was that our next-door neighbors, the Joyce family, had children the same age. Dan and Pat Joyce became good friends, and we soon began "sharing" our children. Their daughter Marisa remains one of my daughter Maddie's best friends; they met when they were nine.

The move was also very hard on me. I no longer had the safety net of my family and longtime friends to help me navigate my roles as an officeholder and mother.

Tom Simon was an institution in the state capital and a wonderful support during this time. He had lived in Jefferson City for many years and was invaluable in helping me get my family settled in. He was officially the clerk of the state supreme court, but unofficially he was much more. He was fatally charming and made friends easily. When I was in the state legislature, I watched in awe as he captured the confidence of every powerful member of the body on both sides of the aisle. It seemed he was everywhere and part of every major deal. He was married to Linda Simon, the executive director of the Missouri Trial Lawyers Association. They were the ultimate power couple and hosts extraordinaire. Their house was the scene of countless dinners, late-night parties, and strategy sessions.

During the months following my divorce, I ran into Tom at meetings related to the Missouri Bar Association. I learned that he too was going through a divorce. He was kind and funny, and we had a lot in common. We became closer friends, and as the months passed, he became more than a friend. He understood me and my work. He supported me as a mother of young children. We became a couple, although from the beginning of our relationship it was pretty clear that Tom was going to be wonderful to date but that he had reservations about publicly taking on the role of a political spouse. He was there for me emotionally, though, during the months when I was running for state auditor and as I moved my family to Jefferson City. When the dog was lost, he drove the streets all night looking for it. When I had tough decisions to make, he was great counsel, especially as I navigated the choppy waters of the state capital. I cared deeply for him, and he became my best friend.

The auditor's office is on the second floor of the state capitol. I was familiar with the layout of the building from my time in the legislature. But the office was unlike any I had had as a member of the Missouri House of Representatives. It was large, beautiful, historic, and I had my own bathroom! I was forty-five years old, and unlike when I was sworn in as prosecutor, at this ceremony I stood with only my three children and my mother; no husband and no father. My dad's dear friend, former Missouri Supreme Court Chief Justice Robert Donnelly, administered the oath. A nephew of Governor Phil Donnelly, the judge, who had known me since childhood, was a close friend of both my parents from their days in Lebanon. His participation demonstrated his affection for my family and his resilience—he suffered from Parkinson's disease and died six months later. Because he was such an independent public servant, he was a great role model for me. And in a way he was a stand-in for my dad, who would have been so proud had he lived to see that ceremony in the great rotunda of the Missouri capitol.

In my inaugural remarks I said I had a very straightforward view of my new job: to be as aggressive as possible to save taxpayer dollars. I promised concrete results from my audits. I talked about my father and described the time he ushered our family out of a restaurant in Waynesville after a black soldier and his family had been turned away. I said my father taught me it was okay to be a loudmouth.

Republican Margaret Kelly had been auditor for fourteen years and had built a very professional staff. But they were skeptical about me. I had defeated their very well-liked colleague, the deputy auditor, in the election. I was not a CPA. I was pretty sure not a single one of them had voted for me. And this was not a group that was warm and fuzzy about change. I inherited an executive staff whose average tenure in the auditor's office was eighteen years, and not one of them had ever worked anywhere else. When they said, "We have always done it this way," they really meant it.

Later I brought in some new managers who had retired from the federal Government Accountability Office, knowing that their experience with performance auditing, which I was determined to institute, would be invaluable. I hired some African Americans for the previously all-white staff and changed the dress code after learning that in 1998 women in the auditor's office were forbidden from wearing pants to work. I recruited Cindy Eberting, a former *Kansas*

City Star reporter, to help rework the writing of audits because audits are a waste of time if no one reads them.

Wasteful government spending was not hard to find. Documents explaining expenses were often missing, receipts nonexistent, bidding rules often ignored. The St. Louis Police Board, meeting illegally behind closed doors, had agreed to overpay their chief and some officers. Members of the state Conservation Commission, one of Missouri's sacred cows, took thousands of dollars' worth of wasteful chartered flights. Bond money was missing in the St. Louis circuit clerk's office. Some public college presidents got hundreds of thousands of dollars in illegal fringe benefits. Missouri businesses overcharged their customers state sales tax and pocketed the difference. Two judges in Jefferson City improperly diverted $3 million to remodel their courtrooms. The state Highway Department spent more than $870,000 on events for the staff, money that could be used to fill potholes. There was so much money being wasted.

The state's "Sunshine Law" also attracted my attention. I've always been a big believer in government accountability and openness. Missouri has a law requiring public business to be conducted in open meetings, and, with few exceptions, public documents are to be available to any citizen, no questions asked. I created a simple survey, not a full-blown audit, to measure compliance. It was typed on plain white paper and mailed to over two hundred cities, counties, public libraries, school districts, rural water districts, road commissions, and other governmental agencies, selected at random, asking for the minutes of their most recent meeting. We weren't asking for state secrets, merely meeting minutes. Nearly half violated the law by refusing to comply. We distributed our findings at the convention of the Missouri Press Association and decided to make our survey an annual project.

Being the auditor gave me the authority to investigate things that didn't seem right anywhere in state government and a platform to disclose them if there was a problem. With the state's general-obligation bond market closed to competition, I could talk about how taxpayers were losing money. When state agencies spent millions of dollars on food for nontraveling employees, I could bring it to the public's attention. I could point out the fact that Medicaid had failed to limit the use of a painkiller that was often abused. I had campaigned on the need for greater protections for the elderly, and one of my audits found that fifteen nursing home employees had records of abusing patients in mental health facilities. That audit also found that it was common for a home to get into trouble, temporarily address the problem, and then get in trouble again. Anything we learned from our audits, we let the public know.

Governor-talk started rumbling early in my career as auditor. Just months after taking office, some Democrats were encouraging me to run in 2000. That wasn't in my plans. My agenda called for me to serve a full four-year term. Bob Holden, the state treasurer, was the presumptive party nominee. He began putting together an organization to test the waters for governor in 1997, three years before the election. Bob had connections to Democrats throughout the state; he had been on the staffs of several state and federal officials and had worked his way up through the ranks. He and I were elected to the state house the same year, and we had survived the budget battles with the Websters. But even before that he had worked with and for many Democratic leaders. When Mel Carnahan was treasurer, Bob helped him raise money to pay off his campaign debts. Bob was on the staff of Treasurer Jim Spainhower when he unsuccessfully challenged Governor Joseph Teasdale for the party's nomination in 1980. After Bob ran and lost a state treasurer's race in 1988, he went to St. Louis and ran Congressman Richard Gephardt's office there. He was elected treasurer in 1992 and again in 1996.

Everyone anticipated that his Republican opponent would be Jim Talent, a congressman from St. Louis County. At a meeting of Democrats in Hannibal, I delivered what a newspaper reporter called "a rip-roaring speech" pointing out that Talent represented the extreme right wing of the Republican Party. Talent was part of a leadership group in Congress that took out Newt Gingrich because he was *too* moderate, I said. "McCaskill's hard-hitting performance is one of the latest reasons why some of her allies have been quietly encouraging her to consider running for governor next year," wrote Jo Mannies of the *St. Louis Post-Dispatch*. "That would mean challenging the anointed party favorite: state Treasurer Bob Holden. While McCaskill has been verbally grabbing Republicans by the neck, Holden has avoided any direct attacks against Talent or the GOP."

The 2000 election contained many crucial decisions for Missouri voters. The state was locked in a struggle for control of two major offices: governor and U.S. Senate. It was also in play in the presidential race between Republican George W. Bush and Democrat Al Gore. I had no direct role in the election; the auditor's office was not on the ballot. But just a few weeks before the election, my name became part of the campaign narrative when a Republican operative publicly compared me with a prostitute.

In his run for governor, Jim Talent had a television ad claiming Democrats had "broken their promise" to public education because not all gambling tax money was going to public schools, as the law required. As auditor, I knew otherwise. My own audits, and those of my Republican predecessor, demonstrated that schools had received hundreds of millions of dollars from the tax proceeds. On September 21, 2000, during a news conference in Kansas City, I said Talent's ad was "totally false," and I had charts and statistics to back it up.

A day later Daryl Duwe, the spokesman for the Missouri Republican Party, posted a commentary on his website. Under the headline, "McCaskill Soils Herself for Bob Holden," Duwe wrote, "State Auditor Claire McCaskill let the Democrats parade her around like a cheap hooker this week in an abysmal attempt to divert public attention away from a shell game the Democrats are playing with education dollars." When Duwe pressed his computer's "send" key to post that gem, it was as if he punched the "fire" button on a submarine's torpedo, but it turned out to be one of those torpedoes that goes crazy, out of control, and circles back to demolish its source.

Duwe made national news and prompted a backlash against the Republicans. Soon politicians from St. Louis to Austin, Texas, were scrambling to assess the damage. It didn't take long for the "cheap hooker" remark to make the Associated Press and the CNN news cycles. When first questioned about what he wrote, Duwe said he had a constitutional right to make such ugly comments. But then he tried to take back the remark, editing his posting to change "hooker" to "politician."

The next stage of the story extended beyond Duwe to other Republicans. Soon GOP candidates were asked what they thought about it: "Do you agree with him?" "What about the use of such language?" "Should Duwe be disciplined?" "Fired?" Then Talent and Senator John Ashcroft, struggling to hold on to his seat against a challenge from Governor Mel Carnahan, began to distance themselves from their party's spokesman. Suddenly the headline seemed to be "Daryl Duwe Soils Republicans over Offensive Remark." The raving went on for a week.

All this was swirling around me and I wasn't even running. When asked about it, I said, "I do know I'm dreading going home tonight and explaining all this to my kids." I did call on Talent and Ashcroft to have Duwe fired. "If you don't," I wrote, "all the lip service about values, character and integrity will be as hollow as the ugly smear made against me." State Democratic Chairman Joe Carmichael also wrote. Governor Carnahan said Duwe had reached "a new low in political rhetoric." Secretary of State Bekki Cook, who led a group of Democratic women officeholders calling for Duwe's dismissal, said, "It's pretty much the lowest thing you can say about a woman. This is why women do not want to run for public office."

Other women rallied to the suggestion that Duwe's remark reflected how Republicans viewed women in general, not just me. It was just the kind of remark that mobilized women to get involved in campaigns for senate and governor. It fed into the theme that Republicans disrespect women. "The sexualized smearing of McCaskill, a former Jackson County prosecutor, by a GOP mouthpiece with an X-rated mentality toward women in politics is an offense that crosses party lines where most women are concerned. Some men, too," wrote Rhonda Chriss Lokeman in the *Kansas City Star*.

Duwe said he was sorry, but it didn't do any good. Talent's campaign manager called Duwe's remarks "intemperate" and "perhaps inappropriate." Then Texas weighed in. A spokesman for the presidential campaign of Governor Bush said there was no place in politics for that kind of language. Ann Wagner, head of the Missouri Republican Party, said Duwe's remark was wrong but that they had no plans to fire him. "I couldn't believe Duwe had been so insensitive," wrote Rich Hood, the *Star*'s editorial page editor. "His remarks went far beyond the bounds of fair political comment and criticism. My second thought was, 'When you go after Claire McCaskill, you had better get an early start and bring your lunch. She is a superb politician.'"

One week after Duwe posted the "cheap hooker" essay, Senator Ashcroft called the remark "totally insensitive and wrong." That same day the *St. Louis Post-Dispatch* columnist Bill McClellan wrote, "You don't see guys throwing their jackets over puddles any more, but still, real men don't hurl those kind of insults at women. No wonder there's a gender gap." The point of McClellan's column was that Duwe was poison for Talent's campaign. Ten days after the "cheap hooker" posting, Duwe resigned. I responded with a one-sentence statement: "He's moving on, and I'm moving on as well."

Daryl Duwe's remark became a small footnote in Missouri's 2000 election. Within a few days the entire state was plunged into grief.

I was working at our kitchen table in Jefferson City late in the evening on Monday, October 16, catching up on reading after just putting the kids to bed. The phone rang. It was Gracia Backer, my friend and former colleague. "They can't find the governor's plane," she said. "They took off from St. Louis but never landed in New Madrid. Stay off the phone." Alone in my kitchen I contemplated the worst. A short time later, which seemed like an eternity, I got two more calls. One was from Roy Temple, the governor's chief of staff, saying the governor's plane had crashed and there were no survivors. This was especially difficult for Roy; he had lost not only his hero and boss, but his best friend, the governor's campaign advisor, Chris Sifford, who was also on board. The pilot of the plane was Governor Carnahan's oldest son, Randy. The second call was from Lieutenant Governor Roger Wilson. He asked me to immediately come to the capitol to fulfill my role on the statutory Disability Board.

Around midnight, just hours after the governor's plane went down, I joined Lieutenant Governor Wilson, Secretary of State Rebecca Cook, Attorney General Jay Nixon, House Speaker Steve Gaw of Moberly, and Senate President Pro Tem Ed Quick of Liberty. We were six members of the nine-member state Disability Board, whose sad job it was to determine that Governor Carnahan could not carry out his duties under the state constitution. Shortly after two o'clock the next morning the six of us signed a statement that made Roger Wilson the acting governor.

Mel Carnahan had been such a courageous and generous public servant, whose political success stemmed from his hard work and genuine humility. He believed that public service could be a high calling. He wasn't telegenic or even a great speaker; he was often reserved, shy, and reluctant to toot his own horn. But he took on controversial issues and didn't hesitate to go toe-to-toe with powerful special interests. He abided by a policy that he often repeated to his staff: "Do the right thing and the politics will sort themselves out later."

During nearly eight years as governor, Mel Carnahan had managed to pass a $315 million tax increase in the Missouri Legislature to finance the Outstanding Schools Act. He generated the wrath of the insurance lobby by pushing passage, unsuccessfully, of an overhaul in health care coverage. Many thought he committed political suicide when he commuted the death sentence of a convicted killer at the request of Pope John Paul II during a visit to St. Louis. He took on the gun lobby to defeat a concealed weapons measure in the only statewide election of its kind ever held in this country. There was no family-planning money for poor women in Missouri until Mel Carnahan became governor. And he courageously vetoed legislation that would have severely limited a woman's right to terminate a pregnancy.

A tragedy similar to Governor Carnahan's death had struck Missouri during a senate race in the recent past. In 1976, on the day he won the Democratic primary, Congressman Jerry Litton was killed in a plane crash on his way to a victory party in Kansas City. His wife and two children and the pilot and his son were also killed. In that case there was time for the Democratic State Committee to meet and select an alternate candidate, former governor Warren Hearnes. But in the case of Mel Carnahan's death, there wasn't enough time before the election to get another candidate's name on the ballot. Governor Wilson announced that if Mel Carnahan were elected posthumously, he would name the governor's widow, Jean Carnahan, to serve a two-year term in the U.S. Senate until the general election of 2002. One week before the election, Jean announced that she was willing to accept the job. "It's a proper way to carry his ideals forward," she said.

On November 7, 2000, Bob Holden became governor by a very narrow margin. He received 49 percent of the vote to Jim Talent's 48 percent. Only 21,445 votes separated them out of 2,346,830 cast. Mel Carnahan received 50 percent of the vote compared to 48 percent for Ashcroft, and Jean Carnahan was named Missouri's first female senator. George W. Bush was Missouri's presidential choice.

By this time Tom Simon had been divorced from his wife, and we had been dating each other for a couple of years. But as our relationship aged, I became frustrated with his unwillingness to step up to a more permanent commitment. It finally came to a head with Holden's election. There is a procession that traditionally occurs at the Inaugural Ball in the rotunda of the state capitol. As state auditor, my walk down the long staircase required an escort. I assumed that this would be the time that Tom would join me in a public acknowledgment of our relationship. But he demurred, suggesting that Austin escort me. That was it. I was done. We broke off our relationship in the fall of 2000. My New Year's resolution for 2001 was to get out of Jefferson City for social occasions because I was confident that I was more likely to find more men who could relate to me and my career in Kansas City and St. Louis.

So as the New Year began, I made an effort to attend events in Kansas City and St. Louis on the weekends that the kids were with their dad. One weekend early in the year brought me to St. Louis for a fundraiser on my behalf. One of the attendees, Mark Levison, and his guest asked me to go out afterward for a drink. His friend asked me about my personal life. I explained that I was single and interested in meeting new people, preferably outside of politics. She insisted I come to St. Louis for her birthday party in a few weeks. "I have a big house," she said. "There will be loads of interesting people there your age. You can have a few drinks and spend the night without worrying about driving. Besides, I want you to meet the man I'm dating. He gives money to political candidates, and I bet he will help you."

I took her up on her invitation. She was right, there were lots of interesting people at her party. The man she was dating arrived late because he was just getting back from a ski trip with his children. His name was Joseph Shepard. Within a week I got a call at the auditor's office from Joseph. He was coming to Jefferson City on business and wanted to know if I would have lunch with him. I agreed because I thought he could be a campaign supporter. I was right, but in ways I didn't even contemplate when I accepted his invitation. He became the most important supporter in my life. As Joseph recalled, "It just worked. I mean it was unbelievable. I don't think I've ever had an experience like that, where you just hit on all cylinders right away."

That first lunch was interesting. He was clearly very smart but slightly intimidating and officious. I wasn't sure what to make of him. He asked me to call him when I was going to be in St. Louis the next time. A few weeks later I had to go there for a meeting, and I called him. He asked me to come to his office and then go out for a drink after work. When I walked into his office that day I saw on his wall framed photos of Joseph with Ronald Reagan, George Bush, Dick Lugar, Kit Bond, and Bob Dole. Republicans all. I thought to myself, *This is going nowhere*. I was wrong.

We dated throughout that year. I learned he had been through a very difficult divorce and had been hurt in a relationship after that. He had four grown and almost grown children. He was confident, successful, generous, funny, and very smart. Through the years he had gone from being a card-carrying, money-giving Republican to a full-blown independent. We fell in love, and I felt so fortunate to have a life partner who understood me, supported me, and loved my family. That fall we were engaged.

Joseph and I were married on April 27, 2002, in a beautiful cere- mony at Lake of the Ozarks. There were no bridesmaids or grooms- men, no best man or maid of honor. Our wedding invitation said it all: "Benjamin, Carlton, Marilyn, Michael, Austin, Madeline, and Lillian invite you to the wedding of their parents, Claire McCaskill and Joseph Shepard." His four children and my three stood up with us for the ceremony after my son walked me down the aisle. I won't lie and say that our blended family has not had its bumps. It was particularly hard for Austin, who for all the right reasons felt deep love and loyalty for his father. He didn't like Joseph, and he and Maddie were resentful of him for taking us away from Jefferson City and all their friends. And it took years for our children to become close. Now I can look back at the beginning of our marriage with gratitude to all—Joseph, David, and all our children—for working to strengthen the bonds of a blended family.

It didn't take long for our relationship and then marriage to become grist for the political mill. A couple of months before the wedding, a newspaper examined Joseph's business interests with an emphasis on how the findings of my audits might be influenced by the companies he owned. It was the first signal of what was to come: that my husband's occupation and ways of making money would be under the microscope as long as I held public office. In this case the issue was the fact that among Joseph's business interests were nursing homes.

As auditor I had been pretty outspoken about the need to improve the quality of care in nursing homes. I said then that my future husband's homes should be sanctioned just like any other if care were not as it should be. "It's harder to paint with a broad brush when someone you love is trying to deliver the best care they know how," I said at the time. "Are his homes run perfectly? I'm sure they are not. Do I know he wants to give good care? I do. And do I love him? Absolutely."

CHAPTER SIX

Reaching for a Dream

G overnor Bob Holden portrayed himself as an "everyman" kind of politician patterned after Harry Truman. But he clearly was not channeling Truman when he threw an extravagant $1.3 million inauguration party to begin his term as governor. Chandeliers in tents, chocolate bars with his inaugural logo, and a debt to pay for all of it saddled him with the kind of image that is difficult to overcome.

But in fairness, in many ways his struggles were about timing and plain bad luck. Eighteen days into his administration, he was forced to begin cutting millions of dollars from the state budget because of the sluggish economy. A newspaper's editorial cartoon in December 2001 depicted Holden as the Grinch who withheld Christmas. His chief of staff resigned after eleven months in office, raising the issue that Holden was a difficult boss. At the end of his first year, his political enemies began to refer to him as OTB, "One-Term Bob." The Republicans took over the state senate in a special election, and when the 2002 election came along, the GOP took over the house with a 90–73 majority. For the first time since 1948, Democrats were a minority in both chambers. With the opposing party controlling the General Assembly, Bob Holden could not hope to get cooperation in dealing with the state's problems.

Troubles mounted, some as a result of his own courage. He issued a controversial executive order expanding collective bargaining rights for state workers, although the legislature had repeatedly rejected the idea. He tried to raise taxes on businesses, the wealthy, casinos, and smokers. Republicans said no. By a three-to-one margin voters defeated a plan to raise taxes for roads. In such a climate it's difficult for Democrats to make progress by blasting Republicans for being against tax increases. Fighting over the state budget, Holden called the legislature into special session during summer vacation. An influential Democrat sided with Republicans in that budget battle. The media picked up on Holden's frequent, inefficient use of state airplanes. The Associated Press found he flew an average of every other day, "a truly jet-setting pace compared to his predecessors."

Then there were the vetoes. His political weakness was demonstrated when some Democrats deserted him when it came time to sustain his vetoes. It takes a two-thirds majority in each house to override a governor's veto. If Democrats had voted as a block, Holden's vetoes would have been sustained. But the legislature overrode three of his vetoes of bills that provided special protections for gun manufacturers, allowing concealed weapons, and requiring a twenty-four-hour waiting period for abortions. Three veto overrides in one session had never happened before. Republicans watched these developments with great relish. They were gleeful about their chances of taking back the governor's office in 2004. Holden was in trouble. Some Democrats stuck with him; others began encouraging me to mount a challenge.

Bob Holden had worked himself up through the ranks and over the years had built a vast network of contacts. He was a nice guy who enjoyed the minutiae of government. For example, he championed a plan requiring teachers in failing schools to pass tests before they could be eligible for pay raises; he proposed that principals in troubled schools attend a special training academy. But he was not effective when it came to articulating his goals. His biggest asset was his ability to raise money. While many politicians loathe calling people to ask for contributions, Bob seemed to enjoy it. When I met Joseph, I learned that he had given thousands and thousands of dollars to Holden's campaigns. When I asked him why in the world he would give that much money, he replied, "He just kept asking." In fact it was the size of Bob's campaign war chest that kept others out of the governor's race in 2000.

Beginning in early 2002 I was getting calls, most of them from Democrats who were scared to death that Bob was so damaged he could never recover. At first I dismissed the idea out of hand. Successfully taking on an incumbent governor in my own party seemed too daunting. Jim Spainhower had tried it against Governor Teasdale in 1980 and failed. The governor has the advantage, controlling the party apparatus, and has the power to make appointments and generate publicity and twist arms. People owe him their jobs. While Bob might have trouble getting votes from many of those people, he could expect loyalty from most of the party establishment, from former senator Tom Eagleton down to precinct workers.

But if Bob was going to lose to Republican Matt Blunt or some other Republican, what good was loyalty? He simply wasn't a strong enough candidate. In 2000 he had won by the slimmest of margins. And that was before his approval ratings had taken a nose dive.

I slowly came around to the idea that I needed to seriously consider running for governor. Probably most influential during this period was Joseph. My husband was my best friend, a confidant, and totally in my corner, and he encouraged me to test the waters.

After November 2002 I did a poll and learned how truly weak the governor was. Blunt led Holden 41 to 37 percent, with 22 percent undecided, and Blunt and I were statistically even. All of a sudden, armed with polling data and a new husband who embraced risk every day, the idea of taking on the sitting governor in my own party became very real. Joseph grabbed my hand, and we jumped.

Here was my thought process: The chances were excellent that Republican Matt Blunt would beat Holden in November 2004. If Blunt held office for eight years, it would be 2012 before I would be afforded the chance of becoming Missouri's first woman governor, which had been my goal since I was a teenager. In the interim I would have to run for auditor in 2006 and 2010. It was a long time to wait. I would be almost sixty years old, and a lot could happen in that time. Overriding all of that was the very bad prospect of a Republican governor with a Republican legislature. Serious damage would be done to the priorities and values I believed in and had worked for during my two decades in public life.

I was on the telephone with people all over the state, and the reactions I got were sobering. It was going to be lonely. When it came to fundraising, Holden and I ended up asking the same people for financial support: lawyers, labor unions, and people like Jim Nutter, the Kansas City mortgage banker who had helped me before. "I stayed with Holden," Nutter said later. "I'm a loyalist. I've very seldom been with someone and then changed my mind." As I made those calls, I shared with Joseph how hard it was going to be to raise the money needed for a primary. People may vote against the sitting governor, but giving money to unseat him was just a bridge too far for most. Joseph never let me off the hook, encouraging me to keep asking. But he also let me know he had my back financially and would contribute a million dollars of our personal money to the campaign. My race would cost him in other ways too. His business operations, even those that he no longer controlled, became campaign issues.

As I prepared to announce my candidacy there was one last all-out attempt to get me to reconsider. My friend Joyce Aboussie asked me to meet with her boss, Dick Gephardt, and Senator Tom Eagleton at the senator's house in St. Louis. I dreaded it, but there was no way I could decline a meeting with those two giants in my party. With Joseph at my side, and armed with the polling data, I went. Joyce began by saying that it was crucial that I back away from this decision. Gephardt and Eagleton chimed in, asking me to abandon my plans. They made it clear that they would be by my side in any future race, but this race was Holden's. I calmly went through the polling data, speaking the language of job approval, favorable and unfavorable, and head to head. Then I turned to Joyce and said, "You need to have a meeting with Holden. The numbers are clear. He's the one that needs to get out of the race." It was tense, by far the most difficult political meeting in my career because Joyce was then and remains one of my dearest friends, and I hold both Tom Eagleton and Dick Gephardt in very high esteem. As we left Eagleton's house Joseph squeezed my hand.

On October 20, 2003, I traveled the state to announce that I was a candidate for the Democratic nomination for governor. My family, including my mother, was beside me all the way. It was an exhilarating day for her. All day long, as we traveled from place to place, I watched her stop to visit with everyone, taking the time to speak to the elevator operators, the clerks at the desks we passed by in courthouses, the waitresses at our stops to eat. I was frustrated with her because we were trying to stay on schedule, but I bit my tongue. This was her way of reminding me that everyone was equally important and worthy of my time and effort. She was so smart, knowing that was exactly the day that I needed that reminder.

The governor's power was soon demonstrated. After the executive director of the Missouri Commission on Human Rights donated $100 to my campaign, the governor's office asked her to submit her resignation. Then the governor removed a retired labor leader from the St. Charles County Convention and Sports Facilities Authority after his union endorsed me. The man Holden picked to succeed him was an official of a union that was supporting him. Some party officials kept trying to talk me out of the race. They said it was impossible to win. But I replied, "I've heard that my entire career, and every single time I have proved them wrong."

And I was not alone.

Bob McCulloch, the St. Louis County prosecuting attorney, stuck his neck out and endorsed me. I got a big boost from former lieutenant governor Harriett Woods, who had supported Holden in 2000; the first woman ever elected to statewide office in Missouri said she was switching her allegiance because I was a force for reform. "It is not an easy decision to support a challenger to the Democratic incumbent, a longtime political friend who has worked hard under difficult circumstances," Woods said. "But loyalty is not enough. There is too much at stake. Claire McCaskill represents broader participation in the party and in government generally."

Public opinion polls gave me confidence. Six months before the primary the state's two major newspapers released surveys indicating that Holden's grip on the executive office was tenuous. The *Kansas City Star* reported that Holden and I were virtually tied, with 41 percent of the voters undecided. In the *St. Louis Post-Dispatch* poll, 55 percent rated his performance as either fair or poor.

I got encouragement from unions too. Union members' views are extremely important to any Democratic candidate. Not only do members vote, but they make contributions, go door-to-door canvassing, and make the telephone calls to get out the votes. On election days their workers help voters get to the polls. My announcement had put organized labor in a quandary. Because he fulfilled his commitment on collective bargaining rights for government workers, Bob counted on the endorsement of the eight thousand members of the American Federation of State, County and Municipal Employees. Because he fought for school funding, he had the support of teacher groups like the American Federation of Teachers. But other labor organizations took the pragmatic view. The Carpenters District Council of St. Louis and Kansas City, with thirty thousand members, endorsed me, announcing, "When the Carpenters Union supports a candidate, it usually means they have picked a winner." The Laborers, the Teamsters, and the Missouri Association of Fire-fighters supported me as well. Even Bob's support from the unions that had endorsed him was not rock solid; many members whose organizations were publicly on his side told me privately they would be voting for me.

There were awkward moments on the road. At Hannibal Days, a big Democratic gathering in Mark Twain's hometown, New Mexico's governor Bill Richardson publicly declared his support for Holden while I was sitting on the same platform a few feet away. It got even worse when Lieutenant Governor Joe Maxwell took the podium and talked about the good donkeys in the Democratic Party, as opposed to the "jackasses that just want to knock the barn down." Ouch. There were hundreds of people there, and Holden got a warm welcome and a standing ovation. When it was my turn to speak, I said we needed to field our strongest candidates, and several dozen people in the crowd stood up in agreement. But it was clear that most people there sided with Holden. My mother was miserable.

In April party officials controlled by Holden declined to let me speak at the Democratic State Convention in Columbia. Prior to the convention, Holden forces had removed from an official slate of candidates the name of Sandra Querry, a member of the Democratic National Committee. Sandra and her husband, Keith, of Local 53 of the International Brotherhood of Electrical Workers, were support-ing me for governor. Sandra had worked for the party for more than twenty years, and I was sick that she was being kicked to the curb in their effort to hurt me. We quickly mobilized our supporters at the convention, many of whom were not public in their support of my candidacy. We worked the phones the night before and decided to try to get Sandra elected from the floor of the convention. It was a great victory when the votes were counted and she had won. Roy Temple, who was managing Holden's campaign, was not happy.

When I did get out to campaign face-to-face, I relished my role as the underdog, and I loved the chance to make my case. Stump speaking may be a thing of the past, but only by getting out and demonstrating that you can answer questions and that you have energy can you prove you are worthy. I tried to convince people with my credentials, and I campaigned like I was on fire.

A typical campaign day two weeks before the primary election had me showing up for breakfast at the Goody Goody Diner, 5900 Natural Bridge Avenue in north St. Louis. People would pause over their eggs and toast to see me working the tables, and not for tips this time. The diner stop was followed by a visit to the Monsanto Family YMCA, 5555 Page Avenue. I believed that north St. Louis needed more economic development tax credits, but instead of the money going to blighted areas, it was finding its way to shopping centers in the suburbs while the inner city suffered. I roamed through the YMCA, visiting with people of all ages and talking about more development and jobs in their neighborhoods.

Between stops I was talking into my cell phone. A St. Louis city employee said he wanted to support me but was afraid for his job because his boss was for Holden. Another call dealt with a request for $7,200 from a St. Louis ward organization that promised to turn out paid workers for me. "That seems high," I said. "What will they do for the money?" At other times I was on the phone begging someone for a campaign contribution, or answering a journalist's questions, or arguing with a political consultant about what should be in our television ads. Sometimes the calls were personal. Maddie wanted to know if she could go to the movies that night; Austin wanted a new video game; Lily was struggling with a school assignment.

When I ran for the state house, I walked door to door. For

auditor, I drove my own car across the state. Running for governor, I needed to cover more ground and I needed speed. Often that meant flying in small airplanes that could easily manage even the shortest runways in rural Missouri. One day's schedule took me to Columbia, where I met with Hank Waters, the cantankerous publisher of the *Columbia Daily Tribune*, seeking his paper's endorsement. He wanted the meeting to be closed to the press because, he said, I wouldn't be as candid. Frankly it doesn't take a closed meeting for me to be candid, but I was more than happy to share inside information with him behind closed doors, including private polling data, our planned advertising attack against Holden, and my frustration with the Holden campaign's going after my husband.

At a fundraising appearance in Christian County, just outside of Springfield, I said that when I arrived in state government in 1983, Democrats had majorities in the house and senate. Now I worried that I would be the last Democrat in the building to turn out the lights. I noted that Matt Blunt said he would appoint a commission to look at ways to make state government more efficient. That wasn't necessary—all he had to do was read my audits, I said. I promised to carry out one hundred of my audit recommendations in the first one hundred days in the governor's office.

After the fundraising event it was on to Branson, where I would campaign the following morning, before taking off for St. Joseph, two hundred miles away. From St. Louis to Columbia, on to Springfield and Branson: it was all in a day's work. Old-fashioned hand-shaking campaigning, editorial boards, fundraising, speeches, and meetings were commonly all mashed together in fourteen-hour days. It was exhausting and I loved it.

The need for campaign cash was constantly on my mind. I did a slow burn over the amount of money Holden was able to stack up because he was the leader of the state party. At that time there was a $1,200 limit on individual donations to statewide candidates, but Holden could take advantage of a loophole that allowed political party committees to give twenty times that amount. He received hundreds of thousands of dollars from unions and other groups that funneled contributions through dozens of regional party organizations. Before the primary election was over, Holden would raise and spend just over $7 million. My campaign spent about half that amount. We provided about $1.6 million in personal money, and the rest came from what I could raise and from what I had saved from my campaign for reelection as auditor.

In an email sent to supporters, Holden's people attacked my husband for the campaign contributions we were making to my effort. I found that galling since Holden was perfectly comfortable with my husband's contributions when they were going to him before our marriage. As Election Day approached, and Holden and I appeared to be running neck and neck, his campaign sponsored television commercials attempting to connect my performance as auditor with the care the elderly received at the nursing homes Joseph had once owned. Yet Joseph had divested himself of the companies operating the homes, the incidents at the homes his company had owned occurred before we married, and Holden had received many more campaign contributions from nursing home owners than I had.

I was proud of my record as auditor, going after troubled nursing homes and protecting seniors. My audits had found that about a thousand people were unfit for the nursing home jobs they held, that hundreds of state inspections had never happened, and that nursing homes increased staff levels just before inspections. My findings led to the passage of a 2003 law reforming Missouri's nursing homes. I had testified before the U.S. Congress on the need for strong protections for seniors.

Joseph was livid. "A male politician's wife is off limits, you can't go after her, but a female politician's husband is the center of attention," he said later. My skin was much thicker than his;

I had been through this before. But Joseph had quietly and privately gone from working in a steel mill to creating thousands of jobs as a self-made and very successful businessman. I thought he would come to blows with Roy Temple after one of my debates with Holden. The candidates were to meet with reporters separately after the televised debate, and as we walked to our news conference, we could hear Temple giving his spin to a gaggle of journalists: "He is the dirtiest nursing home operator in the state of Missouri." At my side I could feel Joseph tense up, then his body went rigid and he seemed about to lunge. I quickly grabbed him and we moved into a nearby room.

Debating has come naturally to me since high school. I know how to prepare and I know how to handle myself, making points with few words. I do not ramble. We were also prepared as a team. We predicted Holden's answers to the issues that we thought would be raised and prepared in advance written arguments that countered his statements. We distributed those responses to the journalists covering the debate, and they took the wind out of much of what Holden said. The papers compared the rhetoric with reality. The debate reactions gave us a good bounce.

We gained in the polls and in our newspaper endorsements. We also had to dramatically expand the capacity of our Internet server because of the high amount of traffic we were receiving. The polls showed the race was too close to call, but the figures were trending in my direction. A poll conducted between July 20 and 22 found that fewer than 50 percent of respondents had a favorable opinion of Holden, and 14 percent were undecided. That spelled disaster for Holden, since undecided voters usually break against the incumbent.

By the end of the campaign, I was running on sheer adrenaline. During the five days leading up to August 3, 2004, when voters went to the polls, I traveled to seventeen cities. On election morning I voted with my family at my home precinct in St. Louis County, held another event in St. Louis, and then made a final swing across the state. Poised for the results, our victory party was set up at the Marriott Muehlebach Hotel in downtown Kansas City, one of Truman's favorites. I felt very good about where we were. I believed I had done everything I could; I had spent every ounce of energy that I had.

According to the Associated Press, it was the most closely watched gubernatorial race in the country. As returns started coming in, I was doing well. We needed to get a big vote in Kansas City and to do well outstate; both happened. I was ahead throughout the evening, and the only question was whether the vote-heavy regions in St. Louis would reverse the trend. That did not happen. When the final returns came in, I had won with nearly 52 percent of the vote compared to 45 percent for Holden, or by slightly more than fifty-four thousand votes.

Bob was holding his gathering at a union hall in St. Louis. He called me shortly after eleven o'clock. "Now I want you to know we are all Democrats," he said. "And we're going to work to elect this Democratic ticket in November 2004." He was classy and polite. I told my supporters, "We have to come together as a party, reach out our hands to all those fine people of the state who supported Governor Holden, that we respect them and that we welcome them to our fight against the Republicans in November."

It was as if I had been climbing a mountain and the clouds had parted just enough for me to see the summit. I was so close I could almost touch it. Three months: that's how much time I had. I had been working on this campaign, directly or indirectly, since I was a teenager. But it wasn't long before I realized that my confidence had blinded me to the reality of what I faced. I was underestimating my opponent. The shape of the national race would bear on my prospects. The time I needed to make peace within my own party was time taken away from campaigning. The time I needed to raise money would keep me from visiting the parts of the state where I needed to build support. All these shortcomings would become obvious in the months ahead.

Bob Holden showed great character by almost immediately encouraging Democrats to unite behind me, and it didn't take long for his supporters to respond. I needed it: the campaign coffers were empty. It was not hard to get everyone on the same page because my Republican opponent was so conservative and Missouri was still considered a toss-up in the presidential election.

But, in the end, being on the same page was the problem baked into my campaign: How could we make peace with Holden and his forces and yet demonstrate that we represented a change from the state government of the past? From day one the Blunt campaign connected me with Holden. "Democratic voters were so divided because there was very little difference between Claire McCaskill and Bob Holden," wrote Ann Wagner, chair of the Missouri Republican Party. "It's time for a change and that's what Matt Blunt offers our state."

Our campaign emphasized my experience as a state legislator, as a prosecutor, and as auditor, and it argued that Matt Blunt was "just not ready." He was young and had limited political and governmental experience. We also pointed out my life experiences, such as raising three children. When questioned, I had a ready command of the facts: I could detail six hundred audits and thousands of findings; I could talk about how to save $25 million in Medicaid and how general-obligation bond issues cost $80 million a year. But I may have been coming on too strong. A *Post-Dispatch* reporter covering my campaign received this email from his political editor: "I just got requests that we address the fact that Claire treads dangerous ground as a female candidate. Especially as she has a rather high-wattage approach. There probably are voters in parts of Missouri who are loath to vote for a woman, but does it merit mention that they'd be even more loath to vote for a woman like Claire? Opinionated, strong personality, etc. etc. I don't know if we can do that, but it's a thought . . . and I'm certain it's one that she and her campaign have discussed at length."

In fact we hadn't discussed it much at all. I thought I was a better debater than Blunt, but it took our first debate to learn that being the more experienced person may not be as important as being the more likeable one. I was talking rat-ta-tat-tat, just the facts, ma'am. I didn't think about how much I should smile or whether or not I should appear soft. When asked what I would do if there were a terrorist strike in Kansas City, I responded that I would call the police chief, who I knew by name, then I proceeded to recite with encyclopedic breadth all the agencies I would contact, names and everything. Blunt began his response by saying, "I would pray."

As we were leaving the Springfield television station after that debate, I noticed out of the corner of my eye the high fives Blunt's team was giving him. That's when I started to realize that my debate performance was not so hot. When Blunt gave the answer about praying my first reaction was dismissive. But much later I heard one woman who had watched the debate say I seemed to be patronizing Blunt. A reporter told me afterward that I sounded like the smartest kid in the classroom, the student who always had all the answers. I had been so focused on knowing the most, being the most qualified, that I had failed to show vulnerability, and that was a mistake.

On the day after the primary, when Blunt promised to be willing to debate me anytime, anywhere, the *St. Louis Post-Dispatch*, two television stations, and two radio stations invited us to debate in St. Louis. Blunt agreed to two, one in Kansas City and a second in Springfield. Some of the political science professors who watched both concluded that Blunt was able to dispel the notion that he was too young. He surprised me, which was another thing I learned: Never, never, never underestimate your opponent.

Winning political campaigns need people in the field to get voters to the polls. Mel Carnahan and Bill Clinton had combined forces on get-out-the-vote campaigns in 1992 and 1996 and were very effective. Running as auditor in off-year elections, I was not as experienced in this area of electioneering. I had key people who supported me. I had friends and donors and people who wanted me to win. But I didn't have anywhere near the statewide get-out-the-vote network that Carnahan or Holden had developed over the years.

What made it worse was when John Kerry, running for president on the Democratic ticket and confronted by low polling numbers in Missouri, decided to pull out and send his forces elsewhere less than a month before the election. I was at an event in Kennett when a campaign assistant told me, "There's a call from the Kerry campaign you have to take right now." I stepped outside and listened, stunned at the news that they were pulling out of Missouri. I pleaded with the campaign operative who had been given the dirty job of calling me. I asked for time to allow us to hire some of Kerry's staff. The answer was no. Within twenty-four hours all the offices were shut down and all the staffers had been moved to other states. Our entire effort to get voters to the polls was gone, vanishing literally overnight. I was numb with worry. There was no time or money to replicate their work. We were in serious trouble; we had to build an organization in only four weeks, diverting a lot of time, attention, and money.

I was campaigning nonstop, losing my voice. Joseph was worried about me. He had words with the campaign manager, the media consultants, and the press people, arguing that I needed more down time: "You just can't book her every day for thirty-five days straight from morning to night and think she's going to be the same perky Claire. Nobody can do that."

Just a few weeks before voters went to the polls, I had a feeling the campaign had gotten away from me. I was in a hotel room in Hannibal, and I turned on the television and saw an ad for me that I had never seen before. I was tired, and I was angry. I had allowed my manager to schedule me out of being deeply involved in the strategic decisions. It got so bad that one day in the closing weeks of the campaign, I went on a "mini strike." I left the campaign office by myself, driving away without a word. I ignored my cell phone and drove to a Taco Bell in the St. Louis suburbs. There, in the parking lot, I enjoyed two tacos and a Diet Pepsi. Finally, about an hour later, I called my campaign manager. "You are where?" he asked, incredulous. I returned to the office and we went on, but the message was sent: I needed and wanted to be more involved.

On Tuesday, November 2, Missouri voters went to the polls to decide who would be president, U.S. senator, governor, lieutenant governor, secretary of state, treasurer, and attorney general, as well as other offices. Exit polling showed that voters who felt safer than they had four years earlier went Republican, and people who were worried about their financial situation voted Democratic. The state seemed divided against itself. Matt Blunt did better among those in higher-income brackets, while I got more votes from those with lower incomes. I built up a hefty lead in Kansas City and St. Louis and other cities, but small towns and rural areas went almost as strongly for Blunt. The suburban areas were split just about evenly. Moderates leaned toward voting for me, while a larger number of self-described conservatives seemed to consume that lead.

My party was staged at the Renaissance Hotel in downtown St. Louis, and I watched anxiously in a suite of rooms as the returns came in. It was a long night. There was a lot of anticipation and hope, as there always is, that the urban vote, which is usually latest, will come to your rescue like the cavalry over the horizon. At around ten o'clock the numbers showed we were doing better in the cities than Holden had done four years earlier but that Blunt was doing better than Jim Talent had done in rural areas.

The numbers that began rolling in from rural Missouri were

bad news. Blunt's margins were so large in outstate Missouri that it would take an unprecedented turnout in St. Louis to make up the difference. I told my staff that I didn't think we were going to get it done. My mother was more upset than anyone. We waited anxiously for the always late numbers from St. Louis City. They were good, but not good enough. It was almost one o'clock in the morning before news organizations called Blunt the winner, and I had to do something I'd never done before: make a telephone call to concede the election and congratulate the winner.

That was a big day for Republicans. George Bush was returned to the presidency; in Missouri he won more than 53 percent of the vote. Kit Bond kept his U.S. Senate seat. Matt Blunt defeated me 51 to 48 percent; out of 2.6 million votes, he won by about eighty-one thousand. Of our other statewide candidates, Robin Carnahan (Mel and Jean's daughter) won secretary of state, and Jay Nixon won his fourth term as attorney general. Coupled with the fact that Republicans retained control of the state house and senate, Blunt's victory meant that for the first time in more than eighty years, the GOP controlled all of Missouri government.

In the days that followed, I pored over the results, picking through the returns of each precinct, township, and county. I compared what I got with the numbers for others, not just Blunt but Kerry and Nixon and Bekki Cook. I measured my performance against Holden's from four years earlier. I put my numbers up against everyone else's. And I studied the exit polls to determine how voters had cast their ballots by gender and age and political persuasion. It was like being back in college, studying political science.

The numbers told quite a story. Blunt and I split the women's vote, which was a terrible showing for me. When I ran against Holden a focus group was asked to compare us to animal creatures; the consensus was that Bob was a teddy bear and I was a cobra. One woman compared me to Cruella de Vil. I also did not run as strong in rural counties as I did in the primary against Holden, nor as well as Holden did four years earlier. Blunt's voting strength was in traditionally Republican strongholds like southwestern Missouri and the state's rural counties.

As I went over the returns, I realized that my hunt for support should have included rounding up independent voters everywhere, not just in the urban and suburban areas. I began to grasp how many independent voters there were and how spread out they were. I needed to quit looking at a campaign in Missouri as if it occurred only along the I-70 corridor. It was not about driving back and forth from St. Louis to Kansas City with stops in Columbia; it was about traveling everywhere I possibly could and talking face-to-face with opinion leaders in all different sizes of communities in every corner of the state. I could not win by simply campaigning to my base; I had to cut into margins in the red parts of the state. I had misunderstood independent voters in 2004: they didn't want to just change quarterbacks; they wanted to change teams. They were not convinced that anybody with a D behind their name was going to be the kind of governor they wanted.

There was a party for my staff at our lake house, with Motown music, alcohol, and dancing. Everyone let loose. It was the kind of celebration you have after something good happens. As we danced to the Temptations, I looked around at all the talented young people who had worked their tails off in the campaign, and I was reminded of how blessed I was.

But never having lost an election before, it wasn't easy to get used to it. After thinking about what I had done wrong, I knew I could do better with another shot. Would I get one? Matt Blunt might be in for eight years. I was competitive enough to consider challenging him again in four. But Jay Nixon had ideas of his own.

Three days after the election Nixon asked for a meeting. He walked in the room and announced that he was going to run against Blunt in 2008. It was bold. For gosh sakes, my body was not even cold, and here he was trying to roll me into my political grave. As a politician I understood what he was trying to do, but I was surprised he didn't have the good manners to wait more than three days. At that moment I felt despair and intense dislike for Jay Nixon, and for the first time in decades I was unsure of what my future goals were.

CHAPTER SEVEN

"Go for It"

The loss to Matt Blunt was a stunning blow, but it wasn't the end of the world. I had a happy family life, a wonderful husband, my children were doing well, my mom's health was holding up, and I was happy that she was now living with us in St. Louis. I had an important and fulfilling job to return to in Missouri's state capital. So many blessings filled my life that after I spent a couple of months sleeping, baking too many chocolate chip cookies, drinking too much wine, and trying not to feel sorry for myself, I got up and tried to get back to a more rounded life of family and friends and being state auditor.

I had never planned to run for the U.S. Senate, but just after the first of the year, I began getting calls from its key Democratic members: Harry Reid, Chuck Schumer, Debbie Stabenow, and Patty Murray. They asked if I'd be interested in running against Jim Talent. He had been elected in 2002, defeating Jean Carnahan, and was scheduled to complete the rest of that term in 2006. In my opinion he hadn't made a big impression on Missourians during his time in the Senate, but neither had he been the subject of any controversy or scandal. He and I disagreed on a lot of things, but I thought it would not be a good idea to challenge him. My first reaction to all the calls? Out of the question. No way. Not happening.

I did think the two people who won in 2004, Secretary of State Robin Carnahan and Attorney General Jay Nixon, should consider running. I convened a meeting at the state party office on the Mississippi River levee in St. Louis to discuss the possibility. Robin demurred, saying she needed to establish a record of her own outside of her family's legacy. Jay had run for the Senate twice and wasn't going to try again. I had hoped Jay would jump at the chance because that would take care of a potential primary for governor in 2008. At that point I was still not willing to see the future without another race for governor.

I cast about, hoping others would be interested. I took Lieutenant Governor Joe Maxwell out to dinner and tried to coax him into the race. He declined; his wife was ill and his family needed him at home. As the months progressed, the Missouri Democratic Party had no candidate in the pipeline for the Senate race less than two years away.

The calls kept coming from Washington. I had my own internal debate on many levels. The roles of U.S. senator and governor are so different. A senator is elected for a six-year term to a position that is entirely legislative and collaborative. The Senate rules by consensus; individual senators have very little direct power except to influence presidential appointments for federal judges and U.S. attorneys in their home state. But there are no term limits, and in many cases the longer a senator serves, the more influential she or he becomes. And, of course, senators can have a major impact on national issues and gain great national exposure.

As the state's chief executive, a governor must be an administrator as well as someone who directs policy. In Missouri the governor appoints all the state department heads and selects officials at the local level when vacancies occur. A governor can serve no more than two four-year terms. The executive has the power to shape legislation, craft a budget, and enact and veto bills. Each state has two senators but only one governor. On a personal level, you're much closer to home if you're the governor.

In the spring of 2005 the Democratic Senatorial Campaign Committee conducted a poll in Missouri to identify the best potential candidate in a race against Talent. I came out on top.

By the summer Joseph had become convinced that I should run. Harry Reid had been calling him personally, with some regularity. Joseph would come home from work and say, "Harry called again today. He may be right. He says you have to do this for the country. They believe they have a shot at taking the Senate." But I still wasn't there yet. I was remembering a sunburned, overall-clad, salt-of-the-earth Missouri farmer approaching me after a stop in rural Missouri when I was delivering some audit results. He cautioned me, "What in the world makes you think you can beat Senator Talent when you couldn't even beat that kid Blunt?"

In early July Joseph and I spent a weekend in Nantucket, Massachusetts, at a retreat for Democratic senators and potential candidates. Hosting the meeting were Massachusetts senators Ted Kennedy and John Kerry and the Democratic Senatorial Campaign Committee. The main topics were fundraising and political strategies. If I were going to run, there were certain resources I had to have. I wanted to be sure I wasn't just filling a ballot slot, that people would be committed to me and not pull out later. And I wanted to make sure that everyone understood we would not put any of our personal money in the race. I was very blunt in describing why I thought I had lost the governor's race and in what I expected to get if I agreed to take on the Senate race. At one point Senator Chuck

Schumer of New York paid me a very high compliment, saying, "Claire, you negotiate like you're from Brooklyn."

Joseph remembers Barack Obama's contribution to our family decision: "When we flew out to Washington, D.C., we met with then-Senator Barack Obama. Barack was saying many weeks he flies out to D.C. early Tuesday morning and flies back Thursday evening. So he was trying to explain what it's like for the spouses and the families. I remember him saying Sundays were off-limits to his official duties. He was putting a good face on the impact the job had on his family. He was a fairly major factor in convincing us to run."

This election would take place at the end of the auditor's term. If I took a stab at the Senate, I would have to leave an office I had come to love. Part of me wanted to avenge the loss to Blunt, and part of me wanted to repay my party, especially those Democrats who believed I had done the unthinkable in 2004. Surely the Democratic Party in Missouri wouldn't survive a three-year gubernatorial primary battle between Jay Nixon and me. We might just end up handing the governor's office back to Blunt.

There was a way that I could be effective on a national level if I applied my auditor's skills in the U.S. Senate. Harry Truman had used the Truman Committee to root out waste and corruption in military spending during World War II. I could do the same, relying on the same tactics I used in the auditor's office. And Talent was vulnerable as a member of the Senate Armed Services Committee. While the military-industrial complex was pillaging the country in terms of defense spending and contracting abuses in Iraq, Talent had stayed silent.

But before I made that decision, there was one person I had to consult. I knew that my husband would suffer most in the race for the U.S. Senate. He had encouraged me, but I wanted to be sure he knew what he was in for. When the campaign inevitably turned ugly and the Republicans had millions to spend, Joseph and his business interests would once again become their main target. What had happened in the governor's race was only a preview. I knew what that had done to him, and I wasn't sure I could put him through that again. We had a heart-to-heart discussion, and Joseph told me, "Go for it. Let's do this."

I knew that once I decided to put my heart into it, how to win the race against Talent would become obvious. To start with, he had eked out only a twenty-two-thousand-vote win in 2002. Polls showed he was vulnerable. He had sponsored a bill that banned some forms of stem cell research, and that was dividing his own party. President Bush faced problems, and Talent, who voted with Bush consistently down the line, would suffer for it. An argument could be made that Talent was weak in fighting for his own state. Missouri had lost three thousand military jobs, many of them in St. Louis, because of a Base Realignment and Closure Commission decision that he did not oppose. He would also suffer from Matt Blunt's poor showing in the polls after he cut 100,000 poor people from the state's Medicaid rolls.

President Bush and Vice President Dick Cheney had supplied plenty of ammunition for me. Bush had suggested privatizing Social Security. His energy policy contained $14 billion in giveaways to oil companies at the same time they were raking in record profits. The mismanaged war in Iraq had become chaos. He was out to lunch when it came time to deal with Hurricane Katrina. If there could be one overarching theme of the campaign it was how Republicans in Washington had lost good old-fashioned Missouri common sense. And while Talent and his handlers would say I had no experience in the nation's capital, I would turn that around to be a good thing: I would come with independence and a fresh perspective.

I told everyone I'd announce my decision before Labor Day, and on August 30, joined by my family, I launched my campaign standing in front of the old McCaskill and Son feed mill in Houston, Missouri.

Our family no longer had an ownership interest in the mill, but the event symbolized something I had learned in my loss in the governor's race. Running against Blunt, I had emphasized my résumé, but because I was a woman, I had come across not as experienced, but as icy or bitchy. This time I emphasized my biography: that I was a product of the country, that I knew Missouri and its people. Our direct-mail advertising showed me as a child, fishing with my father. My mom appeared in television ads saying her daughter grew up in a family with traditional values. I wanted to make sure people knew about me and my family. I wanted rural independent Missouri to be comfortable with me.

But before the year was out, as I was planning my race, a terrible tragedy struck my former husband.

On the afternoon of December 12, 2005, gunfire was heard near the corner of Lafayette Avenue and Seventh Street in the northeast section of Kansas City, Kansas, near a high-crime neighborhood. Witnesses saw a car speed off. The body of a murder victim was sprawled facedown. David Exposito had been shot once in the neck at very close range. A medical examiner said the bullet struck his spinal cord and probably killed him instantly. His body had been pulled or pushed from his car and dumped in the street. The car was later found abandoned, missing its specialty wheels. David had been robbed. Police speculated that he might have been the victim of a car jacking.

That afternoon I was just finishing a meeting with leaders of the National Education Association, the organization that represents public school teachers, in their offices in Jefferson City. I was driving myself that day, and when I got to my car in the parking lot I checked my cell phone and saw I had a missed call from a number I didn't recognize. The voice mail was from a detective in Kansas City, Kansas, who wanted me to give him a call. Sitting in that parking lot on that December afternoon, I dialed his number, assuming he had some request having to do with a case I handled as a prosecutor. But when he answered, he said, "I'm sorry to have to let you know that David Exposito was murdered today." I'm sure he said more, but all I remember is saying over and over "Are you sure?"

I remember very little of the next few days other than an intense and overwhelming need to make this horrific reality easier on my children. I'm sure I made some calls to Joseph and my mother and brother and sisters. But I needed to drive immediately home to St. Louis and tell my children their father had been murdered. It was the longest drive I will ever take.

The years that have passed have not extinguished the anguish I felt when I got the news. Although we were divorced, I still had great affection for David. He was a devoted father to our three children, who were eighteen, sixteen, and fourteen at that time. He was very proud of them, and they deeply grieved his loss. Even though we had gone our separate ways, he still supported me and what I was doing. My heart ached when I learned that just weeks before he was murdered, he had told a friend how excited he was for me to be running for the Senate. David was a very religious man and emphasized to our children that everyone is worth caring about. He often helped the homeless by giving them temporary jobs at his golf driving range. I would not be surprised if the man who robbed and shot him and stole his car was someone David was trying to help. He had no fear of anyone and saw all God's children as equals.

David's murder has never been solved.

The campaign came to a stop for a few weeks, as we planned and attended David's funeral and I spent time with my children, who were reeling. Jim Talent called and expressed his sympathy. I did my best to protect my kids from some of the unfair speculation about their father that appeared in some blogs, trying to tie his death to his getting caught smoking marijuana ten years earlier. But soon it was time to continue building my team for the challenging campaign ahead as 2005 ended.

I shocked a lot of people, especially members of the Democratic Party in Missouri, when my campaign manager's name was announced. Richard Martin had moved to Kansas City in 1992 to run the office of the Clinton-Gore campaign. Later he ran Bob Holden's successful campaign for governor, and when I challenged Bob in the primary, Richard was one of his campaign advisors.

After that awful moment when Mel Carnahan's plane crashed in October 2000, Richard had managed to keep Bob's campaign for governor together and moving forward. His resilience during that terrible time was one thing that prompted me to ask him to run my campaign. Also I knew he'd help me mend the fences with the Holden people who were still very upset that I had challenged him in the primary. Finally, I knew that during the general election for governor, I had lost control of my own campaign and that Richard could help me manage the race so that I could still make the strategic decisions.

I brought my mom into my Senate campaign in a big way. Betty Anne McCaskill became my ace in the hole, especially when we campaigned in rural areas and health care was the topic. The political consultants didn't get her at first, but Mom was raised in West Plains and Lebanon. She knew Missouri's back roads and understood the great people of my state. Mom was authentic and real, no airs or artifice. I also knew her day-to-day involvement in the campaign was good for her health. She had begun to struggle with a heart condition and diabetes, and a political campaign was just what the doctor ordered. Besides, it allowed me to keep a close eye on her so I could make sure she was not drinking too much.

There were times when, in small communities outstate, she got more attention than I did. At one stop in Moberly, my mom shocked me when she interrupted my speech and told the crowd how proud she was of me. "She's stood up to lobbyists, she stood up against a governor in her own party," she said. I didn't know what to say but "Thank you, Mom." Mom told a reporter who was traveling with us, "I call this the dog-and-pony show. I'm the dog and she's the pony."

For this race we took to the road in a leased recreational vehicle, a bus-size camper equipped with a kitchen, a sitting area, and a bed in the back. Wrapped in sky blue with a big "McCaskill for Senate" banner on its side, the vehicle was nicknamed "Big Blue." The RV announced our presence wherever we went, and it became our campaign headquarters on wheels. It accommodated my husband and me, my mother, sisters and brother, children, campaign staff, and political reporters. Our road show touched every corner of the state. If there was an independent voter down a rural road somewhere, that's where we went.

We gave our statewide tours a series of themes. We did a military bill of rights tour with my mom and sisters, talking about my dad and his experiences in World War II. We did an energy tour, an agriculture tour, and an immigration tour. We placed ads in newspapers a few days before we arrived to generate crowds and news coverage. Sometimes twenty people showed up; sometimes two hundred. We were grateful for every one.

On Harry Truman's birthday, May 8, I staked a claim to a role I hoped to fill if elected. When he was a U.S. senator, Truman proposed the formation of a special committee to investigate the National Defense Program during World War II. He had heard complaints from constituents about extravagance and profiteering in the construction of what is now Fort Leonard Wood in Missouri. Putting thousands of miles on his old Dodge, he personally visited the military camps under construction and found it was costing ten times more to build them than had been projected. Equipment was rented for a price that would buy it outright. In just a few months, contractors made three to four times what they normally cleared in an entire year. Truman's committee delivered more than fifty reports that helped the government save hundreds of millions of dollars that were better spent on the war effort. He conducted hearings in a straightforward manner, persistently asking tough questions but without the showboating that characterized some other committees.

Standing in front of Truman's statue in his hometown of Independence, I outlined a plan for what could be a new Truman Committee to investigate waste and mismanagement in Iraq. Military spending screamed for accountability, I said. There was overspending, no-bid contracts, and indictments for bribery. Money saved from waste could be used for what the troops really needed: more body armor, better equipment maintenance, and health benefits. I said our military people deserved better than what President Bush and Jim Talent had given them. This message resonated with people. "She's the kind of woman who could really jerk Donald Rumsfeld through a knothole," said one of my supporters.

One of the challenges was to define my opponent, who as a lawmaker was low-key, deeply conservative, and very pragmatic. Jim Talent came across as friendly and affable, yet the policies he had supported while in the U.S. House were anything but. He had voted against campaign finance reform, against a minimum-wage increase, and against the Family and Medical Leave Act. He voted to repeal the assault weapons ban and to impeach President Clinton. He supported school vouchers. He marched with the House leadership as it espoused a sharply conservative philosophy. So we created a series of ads called "Missouri Voices," which showed average citizens explaining to the television viewer what Talent's votes had meant to them.

While there was a main campaign narrative, this was a race in which subplots could affect the outcome. One of the subplots swirled around a constitutional amendment that was on the ballot at the same time, to legalize medical research using human stem cells. I favored it. Talent's opposition to the amendment had divided the Republican Party in Missouri. Some of the GOP's largest donors were financing a campaign organized by the Missouri Coalition for Lifesaving Cures to approve the amendment. The party's grassroots elements, which included many religious conservatives, considered embryonic stem cell research a form of abortion and opposed it.

In a general sense Missouri's Republican Party contains two groups of people who adhere to different philosophies. There are urban conservatives who approve the party's connection to fiscal prudence and small government, and there are rural and suburban conservatives, made up of evangelical Christians who are more concerned about social causes. The stem cell debate exposed the fissure between those two elements. Early in the campaign Talent shifted his stance, saying he was dropping his support for an "anticloning" bill that abortion opponents wanted; instead he backed a compromise. He still opposed the stem cell amendment, but he didn't help himself with either side by adjusting his position on another sensitive but related subject.

My support for the stem cell issue gave a financial jolt to my campaign. The actor Michael J. Fox reached out. In a TV ad, his body shaking from the debilitating effects of Parkinson's disease, he looked into the camera and said, "As you might know, I care deeply about stem cell research. In Missouri you can elect Claire McCaskill, who shares my hope for cures. Unfortunately Senator Jim Talent opposes expanding stem cell research. Senator Talent even wanted to criminalize the science that gives us a chance for hope. They say all politics is local but it's not always the case. What you do in Missouri, it matters to millions of Americans. Americans like me."

The conservative radio commentator Rush Limbaugh made the ad a major story by attacking it on his nationally broadcast show, and in a rude exhibition of tasteless theatrics, he mimicked Michael's inability to control his body. Sitting behind the microphone, Limbaugh gesticulated with his arms and head and said Michael was exaggerating the effects of the disease on his body. A thirty-seven-second video of Limbaugh's mocking gestures was broadcast on MSNBC's *Countdown with Keith Olbermann*. Limbaugh said Michael had put on a shameless act and that he might be off his medication. This was coming from a man who had once admitted he was addicted to painkillers.

Limbaugh's heartless remarks got all the negative attention they deserved. Diane Rehm told listeners of her national NPR radio show that she had once sat within a few feet of Michael J. Fox and could attest to the fact that he was not exaggerating the effects of the disease. Michael went on *CBS News with Katie Couric* and explained that his body tremors were actually caused by the medicine he was taking. During that interview he was shaking so much that he dislodged the microphone clipped to his lapel.

The controversy Limbaugh stirred up came at a time when my campaign was running desperately short of cash. Using our home for collateral, I had to take out a $500,000 bank loan to keep television ads on the air. But Limbaugh's reaction went viral on YouTube, something we barely knew about in 2006, and we raised close to a million dollars during the next ten days.

While Limbaugh gave me a boost, my uncanny ability to sometimes speak before I think was getting me in a heap of trouble. On this occasion, it all began with a magazine article by Jeffrey Goldberg, a writer for the *New Yorker*. Goldberg's piece explored how John Kerry had hurt my race for governor in 2004. Goldberg reported that I told people in Missouri and in Washington that a ticket led by Hillary Clinton in 2008 would be fatal for many Democrats on the ballot and that a Clinton candidacy would rule out my chance to win the governorship should I try for it again in 2008. "The Democratic Party has to look at candidates who can be competitive in all fifty states," I had said. I was being candid, but in retrospect it was an example of how things that pop out of my mouth can come back to haunt me.

It happened again on October 8, 2006, during my *Meet the Press* debate with Jim Talent. That debate may be the moment in my career when I felt the most pressure. The encounter felt pivotal. I was trying to take out an incumbent who had no ethical scandal, who was hardworking and a smart, likeable guy. I was a significant underdog in the race, and I had to win the debate because it was going to largely dictate how much money we would be able to raise nationally. The *Meet the Press* audience was not heavily populated by independent Missouri voters, but it was heavily populated by Democratic donors across the country.

I had grown up watching *Meet the Press*, and now Tim Russert was required viewing in my own house. As far as I was concerned, he was one of the toughest in the business in terms of not letting someone off the hook. So although I felt prepared for the debate, I was very, very nervous. As we proceeded, I began to feel less so because I had gotten in a couple of good riffs. Then, as Russert always did, he asked a really hard question:

Russert: Do you believe President Bush is a great president?

Talent: History judges presidents, and I think it's going to be . . .

Russert: He's been in the state four times campaigning for you and you supported him ninety-four percent of the time.

Talent: History is going to say there are some things he did right and some things he did wrong.

Talent had a hard time with that answer, and of course Bush was wildly unpopular. The theme of my campaign was that Talent was not capable of independence from Bush. Then Russert turned his attention to me:

125

Russert: Is this a referendum on Bush?

McCaskill: It's about changing direction. I think it's remarkable that someone would vote with the president ninety-four percent of the time and not say, and then not be willing to say he's a great president. Let's be forthright.

Russert: You're having Bill Clinton coming in and raising money for you. Do you think Bill Clinton was a great president?

McCaskill: I do. I had a lot of problems with some of his personal issues. I said at the time I think he's been a great leader but I don't want my daughters near him.

In that stressful moment I was thinking about and focused on independent voters in Missouri, wanting to be authentic, and remembering what I had said at the time about Clinton's conduct. Then Russert brought up the *New Yorker* article.

Russert: You didn't think Hillary Clinton would be a good nominee because she couldn't win Democrats in Missouri.

McCaskill: The presidential politics will get very intense and very frankly, there's going to be a lot of back and forth after November.

Russert: Would you like to see her president?

McCaskill: I think any Democratic nominee is going to be better than this president, and I'm anxious to support the Democratic nominee.

After the debate and the news conferences that followed, my husband and my daughter congratulated me. We went back to the "green room," where my political consultants, David Dixon and Rich Davis, gave me high fives. They said I had done a great job and they were very pleased. But there was some heavy fallout coming.

I left the studios in Washington flying high, but within minutes of getting in the cab, I was on the cell phone dealing with outraged reactions over my remarks about Bill Clinton and my daughters.

It was stupid for me to say what I did. It was gratuitous and hurtful, and there was no excuse for it. And then, to add insult to injury, I had made a huge mistake on the day before Hillary Clinton was scheduled to do a fundraiser for me in New York. Of course they canceled the fundraiser. I wrote notes of apology to both President and Hillary Clinton, and I apologized to both of them in person the first chance I got. My mouth has gotten me in trouble before, but probably never more than in that debate on *Meet the Press*. I am grateful that the Clintons have been kind and gracious to me since then.

At a news conference in Kansas City during my campaign that summer of 2006, I had mentioned to two journalists that I believed Barack Obama was going to run for president and that he was going to win. The future president came to Missouri to stump for me three times at events in St. Louis and Kansas City, and each time I witnessed how he energized people. On the Sunday before the election, he took the stage for a rally for me in Forest Park in St. Louis, and more than a thousand people showed up. Thomas Eagleton, in one of his last public appearances prior to his death, said of Obama, "I haven't seen people want to touch someone that way since Bobby Kennedy."

As people across the country began to believe it was possible for Democrats to reclaim the Senate, raising campaign money was no longer a problem for me, and in the last week of the campaign, I could feel the enthusiasm. Riding in the campaign's RV, I hit seventeen cities in four days. Hundreds turned out even in Republican strongholds like Joplin and Springfield. I almost lost my voice and was popping cough drops and sipping tea to keep it going. In St. Louis I campaigned for twenty-four hours straight, beginning at six o'clock in the evening on the Friday before the election. The campaign bus was crammed with family members and reporters as we stopped at all-night diners, fire stations, and the night shift arriving at an auto assembly plant. At one restaurant a man said his mother had Lou Gehrig's disease and that he planned to vote for me because of my support for stem cell research.

The 2006 elections brought down the curtain on the twelve-year Republican control of Congress. Democrats won the House, as expected, making Nancy Pelosi the first female speaker in the nation's history. And by the afternoon of November 8 it became clear that Democrats had achieved the majority in the Senate as well. Jim Webb won in Virginia and Jon Tester in Montana. Both elections were incredibly close and turned to a great extent on overwhelming disapproval of Bush. My own race was officially decided shortly after midnight. "The Democratic Party once again has Harry Truman's Senate seat," I said at our victory party at the Renaissance Grand Hotel in St. Louis. "He would be proud of the way we did it."

While I was on television making my speech, getting national coverage, Harry Reid, watching with Chuck Schumer in Washington, walked up and kissed the television set. "He has told the story of him giving the television a kiss as Claire appeared at her victory celebration many times," Joseph said later, laughing. As for Missouri's stem cell research amendment, it was approved, collecting enough favorable votes in the urban areas to overcome opposition in rural parts of the state.

I became the first woman in Missouri history to be elected to the U.S. Senate. Yet a woman holding that office from Missouri was not unusual: Jean Carnahan had been a senator for two years following her appointment, and Harriett Woods was nearly successful in 1982. So by the time I ran against Talent, the novelty of a female filling the role had diminished. "She didn't run as a woman candidate, and she didn't have to, and you shouldn't have to," Woods said at the time.

Still, being a woman candidate made a difference with some

voters. Rachel Rau, who lived in Columbia, said I was the first Democrat she had ever voted for: "I voted for Claire McCaskill because she's a woman. We need some representation in the Senate." When I took my seat in 2007, I joined fifteen other women in the U.S. Senate, a record number.

CHAPTER EIGHT

Call Me Claire

Taking a seat for the first time in a Senate caucus luncheon could almost take your breath away. There was John Kerry on one side and Ted Kennedy on the other. Robert Byrd was right across the room. A person could be overwhelmed by feelings of admiration or reverence or even fear. I had gotten some advice from former vice president Walter Mondale, who had once represented Minnesota in the Senate. The job of a senator, he said, could either make one grow or make one swell. I knew I had to keep my equilibrium. I'd seen people go to Washington and lose their sense of purpose and their sense of self. Honestly, if I had come to the Senate at a younger age I think I might have succumbed to all the fawning that comes with the title. I heard, "Senator, you are a big deal" and "Senator, we are here to serve you" and "Whatever you want. You're a senator." My response: "Call me Claire."

I had learned over the years that respect allows you to succeed, and hard work attracts respect. I was determined to know my stuff and to build relationships. If I did that, I figured I could talk well enough to get something accomplished. I was proud to take my seat as a moderate in the Senate, knowing that the middle is where things actually get done.

The big downside to being in Washington was that I was away from my family. I missed my children and worried about them. I missed Joseph too, but I also believed the situation was going to make it easier for us to keep a happy marriage: we'd have some distance for part of the time, which would give both of us room to throw elbows and be independent, and it would also make our time together special.

As a result of the 2006 elections, the Senate had forty-nine Democrats and forty-nine Republicans, with two independents. Democrats had the majority because those two independents, Joseph Lieberman of Connecticut and Bernard Sanders of Vermont, caucused with us. With that control came the right to name committee chairs and direct parliamentary rules. Many people advised me to find a niche in an area where I could make a difference. I wanted to focus on fiscal issues, especially on war profiteering and military contracting. I first asked for and received a seat on the Armed Services Committee. I also sought an appointment to the Permanent Subcommittee on Investigations within the Homeland and Government Affairs Committee. I believed the Subcommittee on Investigations would play to my strengths as a digger. It was originally the committee that Senator Truman formed to look into war profiteering. It was also the panel that Senator Joseph McCarthy misused. When I came into the Senate, I read *Stuart Symington: A Life* by James C. Olson and studied how the Missouri senator handled his membership on that same committee during the McCarthy years. When McCarthy hired a special consultant who had said communism was flourishing in Protestant churches across America,

Mr. White Anglo-Saxon Protestant Stuart Symington said enough is enough, you can't start playing with Episcopalians, and led the walkout of the committee's Democrats.

I was sworn into office on January 4, 2007. Counting all the members of my family and Joseph's, we had fifty-five people there for the ceremony. It was sort of like "The Griswolds Come to Washington." My husband, my children, and my mom had front-row seats in the upper gallery. Mom cried; she was so happy for me. It took about twenty seconds to repeat the oath to uphold the Constitution, administered by Vice President Cheney. My Missouri colleague, Senator Kit Bond, a Republican, and former senator Jean Carnahan escorted me to the dais. I had hoped Thomas Eagleton could be there, but the morning of the big day, he called me and said he was just too weak to make the trip. At that moment, sitting at my new desk, the reality of where I was swept over me. I had campaigned for Tom Eagleton when I was a child; he was revered in my home. Now he was telling me that this day was what he had been waiting for since he left the Senate. This strong, principled, courageous man died two months later.

Bill Clinton was on hand with his daughter, Chelsea, to watch Hillary Rodham Clinton take the oath as a senator from New York. The former president said it was a "happy day" because the Senate had the largest number of women ever. I was so energized to be part of that group.

The first ticklish issue I faced as a senator dealt with earmarks, those secretive, special honeypots of money. My stance on earmarks demonstrated very early that I was going to be independent—not just outside the box, but pushy. Many people in Washington and in Missouri were not receptive to my position. Earmarks are appropriations made for specific amounts, directed by lawmakers to particular recipients. No competitive process is used to distribute the money. Political influence usually determines who gets what. The Gravina Island Bridge, the so-called Bridge to Nowhere, funded in the 2005 transportation bill, was perhaps the best-known example of an egregious earmark. This was a bridge, built in Alaska, which went from one isolated piece of land to another.

Although the earmarking process has since faded into the background, when I arrived in the Senate it was flourishing and few were debating its merits. It was very difficult to track what was going on; often earmarks were slipped into appropriations bills in the dark of night. My position on this process set me apart from almost all of my colleagues as well as the leadership of my party. Once I took that position, I was viewed not as a vote that my party could regularly count on but as someone whose vote could not be predicted. A lot of people tried to give me advice: my staff, Senate leaders, the other senator from my home state, even my mother. It began with the man I hired as my chief of staff, Sean Kennedy. Between 1995 and 2004 Sean had worked for Congressman Richard Gephardt, who was really good at working the earmark system for improvement of the Third Congressional District of Missouri. Sean believed that since my election helped Democrats take control of the Senate, I was positioned to get many slices of the earmark pie.

One of the kings of the earmark process was Senator Bond. With more than twenty years in the Senate and as a member of the powerful Senate Appropriations Committee, Bond had milked the earmarks system for hundreds of millions of dollars for Missouri. The Citizens against Government Waste singled out many of his projects in its "Pig Book," which summarized the "most egregious and blatant examples of pork." There were bridges and buildings named after him dotting my state as a result of his earmarking. Some on my staff believed Bond was a good senator because he brought home so much bacon.

When Republicans took back the Congress in 1994, they brought earmarking up to a science. The new speaker then, Newt Gingrich of Georgia, thought earmarks could help Republicans retain their seats. It became a way to reward those loyal to the leadership and to reward people who voted a certain way. Between 1994 and 2005 the number of earmarks rose from 1,300 projects worth nearly $8 billion to 14,000 projects worth more than $27 billion, according to Citizens against Government Waste.

In one of my early meetings with Kit Bond, he kept talking about "strategic investments." Adrianne Marsh, my communications assistant, was with me for that session. "He kept going on and on and on," she recalled. "And [Claire's] got a slight smile on her face, and she's very deferential to him, there were a lot of areas where they could work together, but he continued to talk about strategic investments, and she walked out of the office and she was laughing. I said, 'What's so funny?' And she said, 'You know what he's talking about? He's trying to convince me to earmark. Those strategic investments, that's earmarking.'"

My staff gave me examples of the best case for an earmark, the middle-range case, and perhaps the ugliest case. The best case was a shelter for abused women that wanted $15,000 for a used van to pick up victims and bring them to the shelter. The middle-range example was a community that wanted streetscape improvements like curbs and lighting to make their business districts more attractive. In the ugly range was a country club that wanted a new building for its golf course.

Although I had my staff come up with a screening process and a way to explain all earmarks I was pursuing on a website so there would be transparency, I couldn't get it out of my head that if I took that step, I would be taking part in what I believed was an indefensible system set up to reward who you are, who you know, who you hire, or what party or committee you belong to. No matter how anyone tries to dress it up, earmarking is not based on competition or merit, but on political muscle. It is not the right way to spend public money. I decided to take a stand for earmark spending reform.

This was viewed as heresy in my state. People accused me of leaving money on the table. The money wasn't going back into the

Treasury, they said, but to other states. My colleagues in the Senate tried to talk me out of my position. As I told my staff, I got called into the principal's office more than once.

Over a year later, when the movement for earmark reform had gained some steam, I sat and listened in a private session of the Senate Democratic Caucus while all the appropriators spoke with sanctimonious authority of our "duty" to earmark. Then I asked to speak. Chuck Schumer later recalled, "In a caucus lunch, where there are just members, no cameras, Claire gave one of the ten best speeches I've heard in my thirty-seven years of politics. She basically gave intellectual arguments why earmarks should go. But then she had the courage, we would use the male anatomy word beginning with B in New York, and she said, 'Look, all you old bulls like earmarks because you keep about eighty-five percent of them for yourself.' It was that kind of thing that is usually not said in the Democratic caucus. She was speaking truth to power. And Harry Reid, at the end of Claire's speech, said, 'I guess the sentiment is earmarks have to go,' and Harry Reid loved earmarks. I'm for earmarks. I think it was a mistake to get rid of them. Maybe Claire one day will come to the view that it was a mistake to get rid of them, who knows? But in the meantime she killed them with one speech."

Beginning with the 110th U.S. Congress, which convened between 2007 and 2009, a number of earmark reforms took root. I joined with Republican Senator John McCain in an amendment that required the disclosure of all the earmarks that were tucked into the annual defense authorization bill. All but one of my Democratic colleagues on the Senate Armed Services Committee opposed the amendment, but it prevailed. As time passed, more documentation was required for earmarks and a better reporting system was established to keep the public informed of where the money was going. A moratorium was imposed, but my office continued to find earmarks slipping in. In December 2011 we released a report identifying 115 earmarks worth $834 million in the National Defense Authorization

Act. Among the requesters were twenty Republican Tea Party freshmen who had campaigned against earmark spending, as well as Congressman Todd Akin from my state. Senator Pat Toomey, a Republican from Pennsylvania, and I cosponsored a bill that failed to pass that would make the earmark moratorium permanent.

Shortly after I arrived, the Washington Post published the work of two investigative reporters, Dana Priest and Anne Hull, who examined the conditions in Building 18 at Walter Reed Army Medical Center over a four-month period. They disclosed a bureaucratic disaster for our wounded soldiers returning from Afghanistan and Iraq. Beyond the findings of poor living conditions in the building, they found that some patients had to wait months before receiving care. I went to Walter Reed to visit a sergeant from Missouri who had lost both legs on the battlefield. Later he sent me an email saying the army's surgeon general and commander of Walter Reed, Lieutenant General Kevin Kiley, had been aware of the problems but had swept them under the rug.

During a hearing of the Senate Armed Services Committee on March 6, 2007, I confronted Kiley: "What I'm going to say is going to make probably some uncomfortable and it's going to be awkward, but I think it has to be said about your command of the medical command unit. In late spring of 2003, the Veterans for America had a meeting with you, and outlined their concerns about what was going on at Walter Reed. Specifically, they talked about [how] people in the barracks are drinking themselves to death, and people who are sharing drugs and people not getting the care they need. . . . General Kiley, you are a professional, not a bureaucrat. And my question to you is, do you have the authority? As the command[er] of the Medical Command in the United States, don't you have the authority to fix the bureaucracy?"

Later I made a direct and public request to Secretary of Defense

Robert Gates to remove Kiley from his command. None of my colleagues joined me, and in fact warned me off pursuing his resignation. On a Sunday morning a few weeks later I got a call on my cell phone from Secretary Gates, telling me he was accepting General Kiley's resignation. Later I joined with Senator Barack Obama in sponsoring a bill, the Dignity for Wounded Warriors Act, which was written to correct the physical and bureaucratic problems that became apparent in the Walter Reed situation. The provisions of that bill became law and it was the beginning of a close working relationship with Barack Obama.

My approach to committee meetings was to prepare in advance by asking for reports that pertained to the topics on the agenda. I knew from experience that there was plenty of written information buried somewhere and that if it could be collected it could shine a lot of light on a problem. To some, these reports might seem like deadly dull reading, but to me they were like a supply of vitamins in the interrogation sessions to come.

Many who complain about government also complain about regulations. They say businesses need to be free of "costly, job-killing" rules so commerce can thrive in a free market environment. But I've often found that what some businesses would really like is a total hands-off policy so they can do what they want. Debt settlement companies, for example: a Government Accountability Office report showed that during the 2008 economic downturn, millions of people went deep into debt while debt settlement companies thrived. They made false claims to desperate people that their credit card balances could be wiped out if they would enroll in their programs. Many people who fell into this trap lost even more money, as upfront fees consumed the money they had set aside to pay their bills. Many were forced into bankruptcy.

During a Senate Commerce Committee hearing chaired by

Senator Jay Rockefeller, a Democrat from West Virginia, I told John Ansbach, the lobbyist for the debt settlement companies, that the premise of the businesses he represented was offensive and that they were preying on people's fears. They were making money while committing fraud. Later the Federal Trade Commission proposed banning upfront fees. I joined Senator Schumer in sponsoring a bill capping fees charged by debt settlement companies. With the passage of Dodd-Frank legislation, the Consumer Finance Protection Bureau (CFPB) began issuing regulations to govern debt settlement companies, so the urgency was gone to pass what would have been duplicate legislation.

There were many memorable moments during my first years as a senator. Among them was when several of us freshmen were invited to Senator Ted Kennedy's "hideaway." Hideaways are just small offices in the Capitol Building, and as one of the most senior senators, Ted's was not in the basement but near the Senate Chamber and probably twice as large as almost everyone else's. It had a fireplace and a very cool keyhole window that provided a beautiful view of the Mall and the Washington Monument, and it was chock-full of Kennedy family memorabilia.

That night the "Lion of the Senate" told incredible stories about his maternal grandfather, John Francis "Honey Fitz" Fitzgerald, who had been a congressman from Massachusetts and the mayor of Boston. Ted called him the family's "consummate politician" and said history hadn't given him enough credit for being as effective and popular as he was. The senator showed us a sword that belonged to Manuel Noriega, the former military dictator of Panama, and a cigar box carved by Castro that had been given to one of the senator's brothers.

The popular stereotype of Ted Kennedy was inaccurate. He was the Lion of the Senate for causes that were progressive and liberal;

there's no question this was true on education, care for the poor and the working class, and health care. But he was also a senator's senator, very knowledgeable about all of the issues that he was working on. He commanded incredible respect from the other side of the aisle as well. I can't tell you how many times over the past several years my Republican friends in the Senate have said, "I wish Teddy were here. He could help us get this worked out."

Just as memorable as the meeting in his hideaway was his seventy-fifth birthday party at his Washington home, when he sang "Blueberry Hill" at the piano. I had a ringside seat and it was a hoot. Barack Obama and Bill and Hillary Clinton were there. This was just before the Democratic presidential primary battle began. Senator Obama had campaigned on my behalf, and we had worked together on some issues. I now had the opportunity to see how open to discussion he is, how he demands to hear all sides of an issue, and how damn smart he is. He is a natural leader and one of the greatest orators in our generation. I thought the country needed him, and I hoped he would become president.

Of course the worst thing a U.S. senator can do is take sides in a presidential primary race. One of them could end up in the Oval Office, and you're forever in the deep freeze if you pick the wrong one. My chief of staff thought I was making a big mistake even thinking about endorsing Obama, much less talking about it to other people. But the junior senator from Illinois and I were friends, and I believed his candidacy was unique in being able to capture the sense that our country was turning the page. Not only did his candidacy represent a break from the Clinton years, it also played to our hope in America that we had moved past our historical racial divide.

Hillary Clinton knew I was considering endorsing her opponent, so she asked me to lunch in the Senate Dining Room. We had a great conversation; once again I told her how sorry I was for my careless and hurtful comments about her husband, and we talked about her running for president. I was honest with her: I said that

Obama had done more for me during the election than anyone else and that we were close as colleagues and friends. The best she could hope was for me to stay neutral.

Several of my colleagues in the Senate gave me a "talking to" about supporting Hillary and pleaded with me not to endorse Barack. The national women's groups that considered my election a product of their handiwork were furious at the possibility.

As the Iowa caucuses approached, I had a conversation with Barack in the lobby behind the Senate chamber. I told him that Iowa would be a pivotal moment. We talked for a while, and then, as he was walking away from me, he turned, looked over his shoulder, and with that now familiar grin and a certainty like the sun was coming up in the morning, he said, "We are going to win Iowa." I remembered thinking, *Either he is incredibly arrogant and naïve, or he has the confidence to pull this off.*

On January 2, 2008, he won the Iowa caucuses. My family had been putting me on the spot about endorsing Obama, particularly my daughter Maddie. She has a way of not letting go when she knows what's in my heart and I'm hesitating. I just kept saying, "Honey, you don't understand. There are big consequences. So many of my women supporters would be bitterly disappointed. You just don't understand." There are two couches in our living room, and the two of us were lying on them watching as Obama gave his victory speech. We were both crying. She got up and got right in my face and said, "I don't know how you can look at yourself in the mirror in the morning. All of my life you have told me that you do what you do because you want to make a difference. The only reason that you are not publicly endorsing this man is because you are worried about your own political skin. If you are truly about wanting to make a difference, then this is the time to show me."

I felt like I had been hit on the head with a two-by-four. It was one of those times when your children have a unique ability to hold you accountable, and I realized what she said was right. I got up the next morning and called David Axelrod, who along with David Plouffe, was chief strategist on the Obama campaign, and told him I wanted to publicly endorse Barack Obama for president. "Just tell me when you want to do it," I said. We did a press conference telephone call on January 13. By that time John Kerry had endorsed him, as well as Janet Napolitano, governor of Arizona, and Senator Ben Nelson, a conservative Democrat from Nebraska. Also by that time Hillary Clinton had won the New Hampshire primary, an election in which women voters played a pivotal role. My endorsement was an attempt to help women become more comfortable with Obama's candidacy. In the press conference telephone call I said that he was "an extraordinary man at an extraordinary time in history."

People across the country, especially women, were very upset. Some wanted their campaign contributions returned. One group told me never to contact them again. Shortly after my endorsement I heard repeatedly about a statement Madeleine Albright had made: "There is a special place in hell for women who don't help other women," and it made me uncomfortable. But you can't be for a woman just because she's a woman; that is just as wrong as being for a man just because he's a man. What we fight for is a level playing field.

Two photos of Barack and me entered the fray and quickly morphed into extremely unhelpful distortions. First there was the "snub shot," which really wasn't a snub at all. On January 28 Barack's campaign won the endorsement of the biggest names in Democratic politics at the time: Senator Kennedy and his niece, Caroline Kennedy. It was a momentous day, which ended that night with the State of the Union speech. The Obama campaign called and said they wanted Ben Nelson, the Senate's most conservative Democrat, Ted Kennedy, the most liberal, and me, a moderate, to sit with Obama as we listened to the speech in the House of Representatives.

Sitting in front of us was Congressman Jim Langevin, a Democrat from Rhode Island and one of Hillary's supporters. When

Hillary came in, she first spoke to Langevin, and then she turned to speak to Senator Kennedy. Kennedy admired Hillary Clinton; they had worked together in the Senate, and it had been an incredible blow to her candidacy that he, Caroline Kennedy, and their family's legacy had chosen Obama as their candidate.

Barack didn't want to appear to be closely observing this first in-person interchange between Clinton and Kennedy since Kennedy had endorsed him. He was trying to be polite in an awkward situation, giving them space for their conversation. So the photo shows him turning away from her and toward me. At the time, we were talking about our trip together the next day to Kansas; he was going to go out to his grandparents' home there, and Governor Kathleen Sebelius was going to announce her endorsement of him. The photo of our conversation turned into the "snub" story the next morning.

The next consequential photo was taken on the campaign plane the next day, flying out to Kansas. Obama's campaign people advised him to walk back to the press section, where he would explain what happened with Hillary. They asked me to go with him because I was a witness. As I was standing behind him while he answered reporters' questions, the camera clicked, capturing Barack speaking in the aisle of the plane and me looking at him "adoringly." That's the photo my political enemies have used incessantly to prove I am a Barack Obama "sycophant."

The Obama people appreciated what I had done, not just taking the risk of endorsing him but all the traveling and TV appearances I did on his behalf. Of course, all that recognition, exposure, and attention had a tremendous downside four years later, when I was running for reelection in Missouri. By that time Obama's poll numbers had sunk far below the horizon in my home state, and my political opponents tried to burden me with the weight of the president's unpopularity by repeatedly running that photo of me looking at candidate Obama with a big smile on my face.

CHAPTER NINE

Boondoggles

Tracking waste in government is not sexy. It involves slogging through records, comparing budgets, making case studies, seeking out witnesses, and conducting interviews. But it's always lit a fire under me. When I reached Washington, I saw that in our war theaters billions were spent on private contractors who failed to deliver. In our most hallowed cemetery, Arlington National, mismanagement meant that while millions of dollars were wasted, families could not be sure where their loved ones were buried. Bonuses went to incompetent federal workers. A program that was supposed to reward Alaskan Natives helped consultants buy Rolex watches, luxury automobiles, and real estate in the Bahamas. Sometimes our system seemed designed to reward these habits. Whistleblowers who tried to raise alarms were fired, and when problems were finally discovered, no one was held accountable.

During the George W. Bush administration, federal government hiring of contractors got way out of hand—not just how much money contractors received but how their contracts were written. Hire a contractor at no bid, cost plus! You can't figure out how to make your agency work? Hire more contractors! We got to the point where we uncovered cases where agencies were hiring contractors to prepare their officials for hearings about contracting.

A large portion of the waste was the fault of the Department of Defense. Our military and its contractors seemed to operate in a carte blanche culture. When I visited Iraq for the purpose of contract oversight, I was told about a contract that was supposed to start out costing $700 million. In one year it went up to $20 billion. The following year, it dropped by $1 billion, and when I asked about it, I was told it was a "fluke." Think of that: a $1 billion "fluke."

In Kuwait, where a lot of the contracting work was done, I finally turned to a general, exasperated, and asked, "How did this happen? How did this get so out of control?" He looked me straight in the eye and said almost proudly, "If I want three flavors of ice cream in the mess, I want it yesterday, and I don't give a damn what it costs." We were spending north of $600 billion a year just on the Pentagon; that's not counting the wars. And where is the accounting for all that money? The Department of Defense has never conducted a departmentwide financial audit, although that has been a requirement for decades.

I learned a lot when I was in Kuwait and Iraq. Most of it would make most Americans sick to their stomach. One of the most disheartening things I heard on my first tour to Iraq, in the spring of 2007, was the admission by many people that the exact same mistakes had been made in Bosnia. After the Bosnia experience, they did a "lessons learned," a study that attempts to find out what went wrong and what could have been done better. And guess what happened to the lessons learned? Nobody read it before Iraq. The same mistakes were repeated.

Another shocking finding dealt with the inspectors general who were supposed to be watching the money. I was not aware until that trip that there is a vast difference between inspectors general in the active military and inspectors general in the federal government. Those in the active military are not truly independent. They report to and serve as the eyes and ears of the commander. They have no fiduciary duty to the people; they are not required to report to the public or to Congress. Frankly it's a stretch of the English language to even call them inspectors.

The number of military contractors spending the public's money with very little scrutiny has grown enormously. For some members of Congress, it's difficult to cut back on spending when their own congressional district is home to a business that relies on military contracts. The contractors' campaign contributions play a role in this culture as well, and there are plenty of lobbyists supporting the defense bureaucracies. It's all part of the military-industrial complex that President Dwight Eisenhower warned us about in his farewell address in 1961.

A component of this culture is the relationship between retired high-ranking officers, defense contractors, and the Pentagon. There is a system in which generals and admirals who retire from the military find jobs in the defense industry; the Pentagon then hires them as paid advisors. The Defense Department called them "senior mentors," but it looked like a conflict of interest to me. The retirees collected nice pensions, pocketed consulting fees from defense firms, and also received government checks as "senior mentors" for the military. The ethics rules that apply to part-time federal employees did not apply to these former officers. I applied pressure and reformed this program.

I also came out against the appointment of William Lynn as deputy defense secretary, the number-two spot in the Pentagon. President Obama said he was opposed to lobbyists going to work for the federal government. But that didn't block Lynn, who had been a lobbyist for Raytheon, one of the country's largest defense contractors. When the Senate voted 93–4 to confirm him, I was the only Democrat voting no.

Some of the things I did didn't win me many friends. For example, when the Senate Armed Services Committee would meet to mark up the defense appropriations bill, I would make a motion that the session be open to the public. Usually these meetings are held behind closed doors, with the excuse that some classified information could come up. But few secrets emerge in these meetings, and if classified material did come up, the room could be cleared. We were deciding how to spend billions of dollars of public money. The public needed to be in the room. I have continued to make the motion to open the mark up to the public every year, and while I have gotten more votes on each attempt, I have not yet been successful.

Contractors now repaired military equipment; supplied food, fuel, and water; built barracks; and even served meals in the mess halls. It had gotten to the point where, in March 2011, there were more Defense Department contract workers (155,000) than there were uniformed personnel (145,000) in Afghanistan and Iraq. And the scrutinizing of these contractors was haphazard. The air force paid a Florida company $101 million, although one project was never started and another was only 85 percent complete. The Pentagon paid Parsons Global Services of California $62 million for two prisons in Iraq before canceling the contracts with less than half the work completed because of delays and rising costs. The military canceled a contract with a Colorado-based company for the headquarters of an Iraqi military battalion because of cost overruns; the company was paid $4.1 million although nothing was built. Examples of wasted American resources were everywhere in Iraq and Afghanistan. The problem was numbing in its scope.

Poorly performing contractors seemed more likely to get bonuses than to be penalized. We gave bonuses to contractors who were monogramming hand towels. We gave bonuses to contractors in Iraq whose faulty wiring in showers may have electrocuted our soldiers. ITT Federal Services International, a defense contractor based in Colorado Springs, routinely failed to correctly repair combat equipment and then charged the government millions of dollars for the extra work needed to get the gear ready for battle. Because its contract called for ITT to be reimbursed for all labor costs, the company was sometimes paid to correct what was not done right the first time. The army paid $4.2 million for the additional labor.

The Defense Department's books were so messed up that our government couldn't even collect bad debts from contractors. The Pentagon was owed more than $200 million in outstanding debt from defense contractors, but an inspector general's report found that the Defense agency responsible for the collections had failed to keep complete and accurate records of delinquent accounts. So the government might have been paying millions to contractors who actually owed the government. With the country facing a budget crisis, it amazed me that this kind of self-inflicted financial wound could be possible.

A valuable ally in tackling this situation was Senator Jim Webb, a Democrat from Virginia. Jim had extensive experience in the military. He had graduated from the U.S. Naval Academy, was a decorated Marine Corps combat infantry officer in Vietnam, and had served as secretary of the navy. He is also a highly accomplished author. We cosponsored legislation creating a bipartisan Wartime Contracting Commission that would examine the problems. He was also my partner as we worked to get the Commission's work enacted into law near the close of my first term. Another key player in the reform effort was Senator Joseph Lieberman of Connecticut, who chaired the Committee on Homeland Security and Government Affairs. Senator Lieberman agreed to create a new Subcommittee on Contracting Oversight, which he allowed me to chair. Once that happened, I was able to better focus attention on these problems.

The subcommittee didn't limit itself to the military but dealt with all contractors doing government business.

Some subcommittee hearings could be very awkward because people were called to account in a very public way. One was retired marine general Arnold Fields, who directed an office responsible for investigating corruption in Afghanistan reconstruction. Fields failed to aggressively investigate allegations of fraud and waste in the spending of $56 billion for roads, schools, electricity, and medical facilities in Afghanistan. Using a no-bid process, he hired a former Pentagon inspector general as a consultant and paid him $95,000 for about two months' work. Only the president can fire an inspector general, and I and several other senators asked President Obama to do so. Fields resigned.

Perhaps the best-known scandal involved Arlington National Cemetery, the revered final resting place for hundreds of thousands of honored veterans. Concealed behind the cemetery's rolling green landscape and orderly rows of gravestones were examples of disgraceful behavior, incompetence, and potential fraud. The Arlington tragedy encompassed all the elements of what could go wrong in government: private contractors paid millions for a job not completed, no accountability by government officials, whistleblowers punished for trying to fix problems. How many other whistleblowers were out there with knowledge of problems and afraid to come forward for fear of retribution?

When self-correcting systems fail, the news media sometimes steps in. In Arlington's case, Mark Benjamin, an investigative reporter for Salon.com, first disclosed the problems. His report led to an investigation by the army inspector general, whose findings were shocking. Bodies were accidentally buried in the same graves. Graves were unmarked or mismarked. Urns containing cremated remains were discarded in inappropriate places. A deeper investigation found between 4,900 and 6,600 graves might have been unmarked, improperly marked, or mislabeled on the cemetery's maps.

This is a Christmas card photo from 1954, taken in the kitchen of our home in Houston, Missouri. I was about a year and a half at the time. *Left to right:* my father, Bill, me, my sister Anne, and my mother, Betty Anne. *(Courtesy of the author)*

This family photo was taken in 1975 when I was in college and our family lived in Springfield. *In the back row, left to right:* My sister Lisa, my father, my mother, and my brother, Will. *In the front row:* my sister Anne and me. *(Courtesy of the author)*

My law school class photo at the University of Missouri at the time of my graduation in 1977. I'm in the front row, third from the left. *(Courtesy of the author)*

In 1981, when I would go to the scene of a fire as the Jackson County arson prosecutor, the firefighters would issue me my own gear for protection. *(Photo by David Hutson/ Courtesy of Kansas City Magazine)*

Speaking on the floor of the Missouri House in early 1988. As the only woman lawyer, it was not unusual for me to be at the microphone on legislation concerning criminal law. *(Photo by Barbara A. Cochran/Courtesy of Missouri State Archives)*

When I was in the State House, Austin would come with me to the Missouri State Capitol in Jefferson City, and I'd often take him to events. He was about six months old in the spring of 1988 when the firefighters gave him his own helmet. *(Photo by Barbara A. Cochran/ Courtesy of Missouri State Archives)*

David, my first husband, and I were in the backyard of our Kansas City home in 1990. Austin is in his lap, and I'm holding Maddie. It was the summer after Maddie's first birthday. *(Courtesy of the author)*

My children, Maddie, Lily, and Austin, and I were at a Christmas party in 1992 shortly after I was elected Jackson County prosecutor. *(Courtesy of the author)*

My wedding to Joseph Shepard in April of 2002 at our house at Lake of the Ozarks. Judge Charles Atwell conducted the ceremony. *(Courtesy of the author/Photo by Carol Patterson)*

With my mother, Betty Anne McCaskill, in November 2011 during my second campaign for the U.S. Senate. Mother always provided invaluable support and encouragement. *(Photo by Alison Barnes Martin/ Courtesy of the McCaskill for Missouri Campaign)*

Making a speech in September 2004 during my run for governor of Missouri at a farm outside of Springfield. I learned at the end of that failed campaign that I hadn't spent enough time in rural Missouri. *(Courtesy of the McCaskill for Missouri Campaign)*

My family—Maddie, Joseph, Lily, and I—were watching returns come in during the August 2004 Democratic primary. Although I later lost the general election to Republican Matt Blunt, this was the night I became the first person in Missouri history to beat an incumbent governor in the primary. *(Photo by Ted Caster)*

Bill Clinton and I were at a rally at the Chase Park Plaza Hotel in St. Louis in September 2006, when he spoke on my behalf during my first Senate run. *(Photo by Bill Greenblatt/Courtesy of the McCaskill for Missouri Campaign)*

When I joined the Senate in 2007, I was one of sixteen female senators—more women than had ever served in the U.S. Senate at the same time. *(Official US Senate photo)*

On stage at the 2008 Democratic National Convention to endorse Barack Obama, I was given a prime-time speaking spot. More importantly, my three children introduced me. Before thousands of people, Austin read from the Teleprompter like a professional. I was even more proud of my children that night than I was excited about Barack Obama's presidential campaign. *(Photo by Gary Otten)*

During the Governor's Ham Breakfast at the 2012 Missouri State Fair, I ran into my Senate opponent, Republican Todd Akin, whose "legitimate rape" comments a few days later put him out of the running. *(Courtesy of the McCaskill for Missouri Campaign)*

Celebrating my victory in the 2012 Senate election, I was especially excited about giving my mother credit for winning rural Missouri. We won the race even before the votes came in from the state's big urban areas. Six months earlier, no one would have believed I'd lead the ticket in Missouri. *(Photo by Whitney Curtis/Getty Images)*

On July 24, 2013, I accompanied President Barack Obama aboard *Air Force One* for a trip to Missouri and Illinois where the president spoke about a better economy for the middle class. On the way back to Washington, D.C., he surprised me with a cupcake and sang "Happy Birthday" for my sixtieth birthday. *(Official White House photo)*

It was a heartbreaking tragedy for families who could no longer trust the cemetery to tell them where their loved ones were buried. The people in charge knew there were problems years before they were disclosed. My Subcommittee on Contracting Oversight delved into what went wrong.

The Department of Veterans Affairs already had a grave-tracking system for its national cemeteries. Developed by government employees at a cost of $2.4 million, the system successfully automated some 2.2 million burial records. But the army runs Arlington, and it awarded a series of contracts to develop its own system, paying between $6 million and $8 million. Some contracts, issued without competitive bids, went to vendors when there was no determination that they could deliver. There was no due diligence to ensure the government paid a fair price. The army officials responsible for overseeing this work did not ask questions that would have disclosed these problems sooner. What appalled me most as a former state auditor was that for ten years there was no review of Arlington National Cemetery or its contracts with private vendors.

Rory Smith, the cemetery's budget officer, had warned the army, the Defense Department's inspector general, and others about problems. Reprimanded and suspended for insubordination, Smith eventually quit in disgust. Gina Gray, an army veteran and the cemetery's public affairs officer, disclosed problems and was fired in a dispute with her boss. At the fiasco's center were Jack Metzler, cemetery superintendent, and his deputy, Thurman Higginbotham. On their watch millions of dollars in contracts were issued, but people still didn't know where all the bodies were buried. Both men were subpoenaed to appear before the Subcommittee on Contracting Oversight.

I was emotional when I began the hearing. The committee room was packed and tense. Unlike most of our hearings, which are full of audits and numbers and very dry and complicated budget management issues, this was a hearing that had everyone on edge. It was a scandal that America took personally. Using his Fifth Amendment right against self-incrimination, Higginbotham refused to answer some questions. In the end Smith's suspension was overturned after his union appealed. He later retired. Gray was not rehired, and the army said her dismissal was not related to the problems of Arlington's management. Metzler was reprimanded and retired. Placed on leave pending disciplinary review, Higginbotham resigned.

The way Arlington's contracts were drawn up and approved turned out to be textbook examples of the worst-case scenario. Just about every document I read among those collected by the subcommittee staff had me saying, "You've got to be kidding me." A later accounting showed that $12 million appropriated for Arlington between 2004 and 2010 was unaccounted for. The army's Criminal Investigation Command and the FBI launched a criminal investigation into possible fraud and falsification of records. Many of the cemetery leaders were replaced. President Obama signed into law my bill that requires the secretary of the army to be accountable to Congress for the cemetery's operations.

I also worked at reforming the Alaskan Native Corporations (ANCs) program, which was supposed to bring prosperity to the indigenous people of our forty-ninth state. But it became a broken program. Instead of helping Native Alaskans, the lucrative no-bid contracts lined the pockets of people living in northern Virginia. People there would actually "rent" an ANC to get contracts because the ANCs have special protections compared with others doing business with the government. The program was effective for neither the people of Alaska nor the taxpayers. So I was successful in amending the 2009 Defense Authorization Bill to stop ANCs from winning Defense Department contracts of unlimited value without any competition. Then I put in a bill to take away all of the ANCs' special benefits: no more no-bid contracts for any federal project. The ANCs were furious and successfully fought back by using the Alaska senators to block the effort.

Next to the Department of Defense, one of the biggest government agencies is the General Services Administration, which manages federal buildings across the country. I was drawn to look at the GSA beginning in 2010 because it had signed a $234,000 emergency public relations contract to deal with negative publicity surrounding a pollution problem at a Kansas City government complex. How many other federal agencies were blowing taxpayer money to spruce up their public image? With a little investigation, I learned that in one year federal agencies spent $1.3 billion on advertising and public relations.

The GSA was a mess. Between 2008 and 2012 it gave more than $1 million in bonuses to eighty-four employees who were under investigation from the agency's own inspector general. A supervisor who had been reprimanded for interfering with an investigation received $20,000 extra in his pay envelope. An employee who was reassigned because of allegations of abuse of authority received more than $38,000 in bonuses. It was ridiculous.

The GSA spent more than $822,000 on a conference for three hundred employees in Las Vegas. Those who planned the conference received bonuses for as much as $1,500 just for putting the event together. The agency used government purchase cards to buy more than $430,000 worth of iPods, digital cameras, and gift cards for employees as part of an incentive program. The fallout from the conference scandal cost eleven GSA employees their jobs. Others were reprimanded, suspended, or received letters of admonishment. GSA administrator Martha Johnson resigned under pressure, and her deputy, Bob Peck, was fired.

In 2012, near the end of my first term in the Senate, all of the hard work on wartime contracting resulted in the final passage of the Comprehensive Contingency Contracting Reform Act of 2012. Under the law, contractors who are charged or indicted for crimes are automatically suspended from the government payroll. The amount of time a contract is in force is limited, and much more must be disclosed: more reporting of contract awards, contractor personnel, contract costs, performance data, and suspension and debarment actions. I didn't get everything I wanted, but it is the first substantial overhaul of the federal government's wartime contracting practices since World War II. I hope I did Harry Truman proud.

I believed my performance during my first term in the Senate fulfilled a promise I had made to Missouri voters to be a good steward of taxpayer dollars. There is a lot of anger focused on government these days—"big government," some call it—like it's the enemy. *We citizens* are the government, and we have to expend the energy to make sure it works efficiently and carries out the services we all need for a better life. Government is not always the answer and must be accountable, but government is not the enemy.

One of my best days in the Senate occurred because of a phone call. Margaret Daum, my staff director on the Contracting Oversight Subcommittee, related the following: A staff member of the Congressional Research Office had taken a civilian assignment for duty in Afghanistan. He had just returned to his job in the capitol after months in Afghanistan and thought I would appreciate this story, which he relayed to Margaret in a telephone conversation on October 4, 2011. He was sitting in on a meeting with military personnel in Afghanistan discussing the need to acquire some goods and services. Someone suggested that it might be possible to do a no-bid contract. At that suggestion, one of the high-ranking military officers in the room said, "Better not. If we do that, McCaskill will be all over it." Talk about making my day.

I had burnished a brand as a government reformer. That's what made it so painful and embarrassing not long afterward, when a serious mistake in my taxes threatened to fatally damage my political career.

CHAPTER TEN

Dark Money

My husband and I were in the East Room of the White House for a St. Patrick's Day reception when I became physically ill. It was March 17, 2011. I thought I was going to throw up. I told Joseph, "I can't stay. We've got to leave."

Weighing on my mind, a burden unlike anything I'd ever carried, was the knowledge that tens of thousands of dollars in property taxes had gone unpaid on an airplane belonging to Joseph's company. I had used that plane for political and government work, and I just knew in my gut there was going to be a blow-up unlike any I'd ever had in my career.

What could be worse than not paying taxes? It was hard to imagine that we would have enough wealth to acquire a plane but not have the expertise to make sure that we dotted all the *i*'s and crossed all the *t*'s in our obligation to the government.

The tax issue had been lying there for years, like a long-buried unexploded bomb. It was unearthed during an intensive self-examination involving everything connected with the plane. The need for that review became obvious earlier that month after Politico reported that I had taken eighty-nine government-business flights on the plane, and they were reimbursed by my Senate office budget. This was not improper or illegal. We did all of that appropriately and under the rules.

I had been very careful about not flying too much, checking on how often Jim Talent and Kit Bond had chartered planes and how much they had spent from their budgets on travel. In four years I flew as much as Bond charged the government in one year. Both Talent and Bond used chartered services a lot. I was measuring my flights and how many taxpayer dollars were being spent against theirs and felt very comfortable that I was being prudent.

But the fact that federal reimbursement for the plane's use was going to Joseph's company, not some other charter operation, gave the appearance that his company's aircraft was being subsidized with government money. A claim could be made that I was using the government to support the ownership of the private plane. Joseph and I agreed that we would write a check for the entire amount of travel that had been billed to the government even though there was nothing illegal or in violation of ethics rules with the way we had used or been reimbursed for the official travel. I erroneously assumed that the reimbursement would make the story go away in one cycle. So we paid the U.S. Treasury $88,000, meaning that we had personally paid for all my government-related trips on that airplane.

Unfortunately the story did not go away because we did not know all of the facts. We got a call from a journalist within days asking about one flight that was taken March 3, 2007, between St. Louis and Hannibal, asking us to explain how that was official since it coincided with the Democratic Party's annual Hannibal Days. The cost of the trip, $1,220, had already been reimbursed to the government as part of the $88,000 refund. The error over the flight bill occurred early in my term, as we were moving into permanent Senate offices. The invoice had inadvertently been sent to Washington before we had a system in place for reviewing such bills. It was paid by mistake. If it had been reviewed, someone on the staff would have said, "No, no, this goes to the campaign." But it was paid, so obviously we didn't catch it. I was beyond embarrassed.

It made me wonder what else had slipped through the cracks. So I ordered a complete audit of the use of the airplane. We pulled each manifest and every document surrounding the use of the plane, trying to find out whether there was anything else that had not been done exactly right. I didn't want any more embarrassing surprises.

We had believed there was no personal property tax owed on the plane because it had been housed in a hangar in Illinois, where there is no such tax on airplanes. But just before Joseph and I left for the St. Patrick's party at the White House, our lawyer called and told Joseph that personal property taxes were owed because the plane had been moved from Illinois to Missouri. Taxes were owed from the time that move occurred. The minute I learned of this mistake I knew it was going to create a firestorm. It had all the makings of the sexiest story imaginable. The last thing I felt like doing was making small talk over corned beef and beer, even at the White House. I was in a very bad place emotionally, and I called Chuck Schumer when I got back home. It might have been the emotion of the moment, but I said to him, "Maybe I need to resign."

Schumer is one of my closest friends in the Senate. He was beside himself because he could tell I was hurting. But as a senator and a very tactical politician, he was busy figuring out all of the ramifications and potential repairs. How do I handle this? How do I work this out? He went crazy when I talked about resigning. He also babysat me throughout that weekend. He has a very calm voice. "People are going to see what this is," he assured me. "You are owning it. Your election will not be decided on this. It will be decided on whether or not people have jobs. You know the people who are going to make the most noise about this are not the people who are ever going to vote for you anyway. Stay calm."

I was angry and disappointed that this had occurred, and frustrated with Joseph's legal and accounting team, but I knew Joseph felt terrible, and I knew that it was critical that I take complete responsibility for the mistake. So, I didn't dwell on my frustration with the fact that it had occurred.

The following Monday afternoon I organized a telephone conference call with the news media in Missouri and Washington. With a huge lump in my throat, a knot in my stomach, and my heart pounding, I explained how the original disclosures had caused me to take a closer look, and a careful review had found that while all sales taxes that were owed had been paid, the personal property tax had not.

"I take full responsibility for the mistake. According to the estimates that I am able to calculate by publicly available information, the taxes that are owed are as follows: 2007, $72,789.74; for 2008, $74,698.53; for 2009, $69,394.13; for 2010, $70,401.01. Let me finally say, I have convinced my husband to sell the damn plane. He has hired a broker, and I can tell you I will not be setting foot on the plane ever again."

This news conference launched a week of unfavorable stories and ignited a lot of speculation about whether I could survive politically. It was as if I had thrown myself on the mercy of the court of public opinion. The chatter was loudest within the Washington Beltway, while the reaction was more muted back in Missouri. Among my friends and focus groups back home, the reaction was "She must be really mad at her husband" and "I bet she's furious." There seemed to be a sense that this really wasn't me, that someone other than me had made this mistake. One woman told my college roommate, "You know, it's a bad mistake, but it's not like she tried to dance around it. You know, she owned it."

One poll showed my numbers hadn't moved a nickel; three later statewide polls confirmed this. I was so happy to get this gut-wrenching crisis behind me. But to be honest, it unfolded during a time when I was undergoing a lot of self-examination. I was struggling over the idea of running again. When I ran for the Senate the first time, I knew it was going to be difficult. I had just come off a high-profile statewide campaign that was brutal, negative, and unfair in many ways. But at that time I thought the end result outweighed the painful hassle: I'd have a job that would be incredibly fulfilling. My perception then was that membership in the U.S. Senate would put me in a position where I'd be able to forge compromises, solve big problems, and touch many different areas of policy that interested me.

But since coming to Washington, I had learned that moderation is not in vogue in the hyperpartisan Congress of today. When I first got to the Senate, there was a stable of moderate Republicans, but they began to disappear. Bob Bennett, a conservative Utah Republican who was also willing to work across the aisle, was denied a place on the GOP ballot by the Tea Party movement in 2010. He was criticized for his support of the Bush administration's bank bailout. Dick Lugar, a Republican from Indiana, was later defeated in a primary by another Tea Party–backed opponent. Other moderates, like one of my favorites, Olympia Snowe from Maine, decided to hang it up.

When I campaigned in 2006, the donor community frankly wasn't focused on my moderate views; they embraced me without much scrutiny because Democrats had been in the desert and people across the country were so eager to capture the majority in the Senate. Fast-forward through 2008, and Obama got elected, and now that donor community has become more rigid ideologically. I'm referring to wealthy people who don't live in Missouri, who've never been to Missouri, and who don't understand Missouri. They have no patience with the fact that I am a moderate and don't see things the way they do.

In the summer of 2011 I went to the White House to have lunch with the president. We ate in his private dining room just off the Oval Office, just the two of us. Over his hamburger and my salad, we began with personal small talk about our families. I then posed this question to him: "What would you think if I didn't run? Because I'm thinking about not running." So we had a heart-to-heart about my plans. He said I had to decide whether I could win, and I had to be honest with myself about that. He told me that, though I thought I wanted to walk away because it was so hard, we still had work to do. We talked in depth about 2012, his race and mine.

I did tell him that if he came to campaign in Missouri on my behalf, it would be really helpful if he didn't say, as he did when he was campaigning for Robin Carnahan once before, "I need another vote," implying that Robin would do his bidding. "What were you thinking?" I asked him. He responded, "I was having a bad day." Smiling, he added, "If I came out to campaign for you, I would tell them you can be a real pain, which is completely true."

At the time of our discussion, the Missouri candidates who had stepped up to seek the Republican nomination for the U.S. Senate were not first-stringers. The first to announce was Sarah Steelman, the wife of David Steelman, my law school classmate. She announced her candidacy in the weeks following the 2010 elections. She figured that she was a good fit for the Tea Party, which had done very well in Missouri, and that her early firm announcement would keep others out. She had been a state senator and a state treasurer and had failed to win the party's governor nomination in 2008.

After my problem with the airplane and its taxes emerged, U.S. Representative Todd Akin said he was running. Akin had never sought statewide office before. In fact he hadn't been in a real race since his first primary in his St. Louis County congressional district. He didn't understand how hard it was going to be to run statewide as a founding member of the congressional Tea Party caucus.

The third candidate was John Brunner, whose family had

started a company that now made hand sanitizer. He was a Pat Buchanan kind of guy, a libertarian type, and he had deep pockets. He told people he was prepared to self-fund his campaign to the tune of $7 million. When he finally announced in the fall, he immediately began sponsoring television commercials that showed photos of me with the president while an announcer blamed us for the national debt.

I decided that what the president had told me was correct: I couldn't walk away. If I thought there was another Democrat who could win, I probably wouldn't have run. But the idea that I would give my seat to any one of these three scared me. They would be elected on no better argument than "The government is the enemy." Plus, after thirty years in public life, was I to turn over an office to a bunch of people who don't believe in *evolution*? I just couldn't do it. If they were to take over, it would be over my dead and lifeless body.

Since I had run in 2006, the U.S. Supreme Court, in its worst decision in my lifetime, ruled in *Citizens United* that anonymous moneyed interests could spend as much as they wanted to elect whomever they wanted. The groups that lined up against me were Karl Rove's Crossroads GPS, David and Charles Koch's Americans for Prosperity, the U.S. Chamber of Commerce, and the 60-Plus Association, an advocacy group that cast itself as the conservative alternative to the AARP. No one is sure who is writing their checks. In the year between July 2011 and the Republican primary election in August 2012, these groups spent nearly $10 million on the airwaves in Missouri to defeat me. Coordinating these ads with a political candidate was prohibited, but in my election it didn't matter. The ads the shadowy groups sponsored were merely designed to trash my approval ratings. It made no difference to them whether their strategy helped Todd Akin, John Brunner, or Sarah Steelman. The only thing that mattered was that I was taken out.

The most amusing thing about these ads was the images. I'm used to people approaching me to talk not about my job but how I look. Not a week goes by that someone doesn't walk up to me in the grocery store or at the airport and say, "You look so much better in person than you do on TV." The images they use in negative advertising are over-the-top awful. I would go out on the campaign trail and people would be shocked by my appearance. They would say, "Hey, you look good! Nothing like those fat and ugly pictures of you that we see on television." And I told them, "My mom keeps asking for Karl Rove's telephone number because she wants to call him and say, 'It's one thing if you're going to trash my daughter, but do you have to use the most ugly pictures you can possibly find of her to do it? Can't you use a decent picture?'"

Over time the relentless drumbeat had its desired effect. My approval ratings began to fall. As 2012 began, the news media labeled me "the most endangered incumbent in the Senate."

I had to do something to confront the "dark money" that had waged a battle against me before I even had an opponent. I decided to face them head-on with a series of campaign commercials on radio and television. The script we decided on began, "They're not from around here, spending millions to attack and attack. But what they're doing to Claire McCaskill is nothing compared to what their special-interest agenda will do to you." It was an unorthodox approach, going after faceless, nameless, shadowy characters trying to influence a Missouri election. We had other ads as well, such as one that said, "They just keep coming back, secret money attacking Claire McCaskill; these big oil and insurance companies don't want you to know who they are." We showed snippets of the Republican candidates' commercials and accompanied these with audio that said, "Claire McCaskill will fight them. Always has, always will."

These were my first broadcast ads of the reelection campaign, and not everyone on my team thought they were a good idea. We were moving precious money out the door early in the campaign and using an unproven strategy. How could our message resonate with voters who would not go to the polls until November? My hope was that if we could help people figure out what was going on, they would be turned off by the messages.

My pushback made national news and led to a *New York Times* editorial, which led to an invitation to appear on *The Colbert Report* on Comedy Central. In early May I was in the studio, sitting beside Stephen Colbert, with an even bigger megaphone with which to blast the dirty dark money. "All these good men want to do is run attack ads against you with money that is untraceable!" Colbert protested. "Why do you have to make that ugly?"

"I certainly expect attack ads and commercials, but what I don't expect is for all this to be secret," I replied. "So we're trying to fight back, Stephen." The appearance led to a significant increase in the money we were able to raise online.

The Republicans' campaigns were inept. Sarah Steelman didn't know what the Violence against Women Act was. Both Todd Akin and she were confused about the current federal minimum wage. Brunner blamed Steelman for an increase in the state treasurer's budget, when in fact the amount reflected how much more Steelman was returning to people in unclaimed property. The Republican primary had turned into somewhat of a farce.

Of the three, Brunner seemed the most worrisome. He was a blank slate with no record, and his assets were pegged somewhere between $26 million and $108 million. For gosh sakes, he had over a million in gold bullion, which demonstrated wealth and weirdness at the same time. On the other hand, Akin appeared to be the weakest. It was time for me to figure out how to help Todd Akin become the Republican nominee for the U.S. Senate.

CHAPTER ELEVEN

Operation Dog Whistle

M y campaign was dealt a blow when I was told there would be no national help with funding the field operation that reaches out to voters. This bad news came from Jim Messina, the deputy White House chief of staff and later the manager of President Obama's reelection campaign. He told me and the other members of the Senate Democratic Caucus that the Obama campaign would be spending millions of dollars on campaign infrastructure in each state where Obama planned to be competitive. Missouri was not on his list.

At the end of his explanation, I left the room briefly, my eyes welling up, as frustration overwhelmed me. *Holy cow,* I thought. *How unfair is this?* The senators who never endorsed Obama, who didn't take big risks in the 2008 primary, who didn't travel the country and do umpteen television debates on his behalf are going to get their field organizations completely taken care of, and I'm not going to get squat. I wandered back in after I had calmed down and stood at the back of the room until Messina had finished. I approached him and tried to calmly make my case. "Let me see if I understand this. I stuck my neck way out, I took huge risks, I have been loyal, and I am his proven friend, and you guys are not going to lift a finger in Missouri?" It was an awkward moment. He looked me straight in the eye and said, "Claire, can we win in Missouri?" Point made. If I were running Obama's campaign, I absolutely wouldn't come to Missouri under any circumstances.

To finance my campaign, including the get-out-the-vote door-to-door operation, I had to raise about $40,000 every day. The pressure was intense. When I walked out of the grocery store one day, a woman walked up to me in the parking lot, grabbed me by the arm, and said, "Claire, you're doing a great job. You hang in there. You're going to win. We want you back." And all I could think of was *I wonder if she has any money. And if so, I wonder how much? And how much should I ask for, and should I do it here in the parking lot?* I even contemplated carrying around one of those gadgets on my smartphone for swiping credit cards, so that when I ran into people, I could say, "Would you like to give fifty dollars? I take credit cards." Of course I resisted that temptation, but the fact that it crossed my mind is indicative of the all-encompassing need for campaign contributions in major elections.

When I telephoned people to ask for money, I had several voices to make my pitch. There's the rat-a-tat-tat voice when I'm hammering information; there's the deep foreboding voice when I attempt to mimic political opponents; there's the really soft voice when I need someone to pay particularly close attention to what I'm saying; and there's the persuasive, saleslady voice, especially at the end of the month, when we're closing in on a budget number and we have to have a certain amount to reach that quarter's goal.

"I'm just checking in and telling you that I love you," I said to a man in Texas who was putting together a fundraiser there.

"I'm one of the endangered species this cycle," I said to a woman in Philadelphia. "Could I stop in and see you while I'm in town? Just to get acquainted."

Sometimes people on the other end of the line would ask me about the lay of the land in Missouri, to which I responded with the same assessment: "In sixty seconds, I'll just tell you that I've got three people running on the other side. They are all just a step short of crazy. One of them said his biggest priority is to make sure we get the UN off American soil, and he's supposed to be the moderate. But let's just put it on the table here: it doesn't matter who wins, this is going to be a rip-roarin' nail-biter."

While face-to-face encounters and making calls on the telephone were still the two best ways to raise money, the Internet had grown in importance as an effective supplement. And there was no better way to use it than to launch a solicitation based on some public development that could draw attention to the contrasts between my candidacy and those of my opponents. Rush Limbaugh's remarks about the Michael J. Fox commercial had helped me raise money in 2006, and he obliged again six years later. In the spring of 2012 Limbaugh referred to Sandra Fluke, a student at Georgetown Law School, as a "slut" after she attempted to testify before a House committee in favor of insurance coverage for contraceptives. Republicans on the committee refused to grant her a hearing, so she spoke only to Democrats. At about the same time, on another radio program, Limbaugh went on another tirade, calling me a "commie babe liberal."

Privately I was thrilled Limbaugh had said what he did. It helped identify him as a standard-bearer for the far right and showcased my campaign as being about the moderates versus the extremists. During my first Senate term, the *National Journal* had ranked all members of Congress along a spectrum from most liberal to most conservative, based on their votes. I came in at number fifty, exactly in the middle. If that's a "commie babe liberal," it demonstrated without question how far to the right were figures like Rush Limbaugh, Todd Akin, Sarah Steelman, and John Brunner. We could use Limbaugh's words to mobilize women and raise money—and we did.

A conversation with my mom about the "war on women" stays with me to this day. I'd returned home from campaigning, and even though it was late, I went to Mom's room for a visit. We watched the ten o'clock news together while I kicked my shoes off and rubbed my feet. The television was blaring away and the people on the screen were talking about access to contraception and health care. My mom looked up and said, "Honey, I'm so sorry."

"What in the world are you sorry about, Mom?" I asked.

"I thought the battle over birth control had been waged thirty years ago," she told me. "I fought that battle for you. I thought it was over. I thought we had won."

During the first week of July 2012, one month before Republicans nominated their candidate for the U.S. Senate, I directed my campaign to go into the field to take a poll of Republicans in Missouri. This was a first for me; never before had I paid $40,000 to a pollster to find out what was on the minds of voters who were never going to vote for me. But this election called for an unusual strategy.

Our poll questioned Republicans about the three people seeking to run against me. At the onset, Brunner led at 39 percent, with Akin at 17, and Steelman at 15. Then we gave the people we were polling a synopsis of each candidate's message. The results were fascinating.

Akin's message essentially stated that he was one of the most conservative members of Congress; had consistently voted against government spending and debt; had opposed the Wall Street bailout, the federal stimulus, and the rescue of the automobile companies;

had voted no on Obamacare; and was a founding member of the Tea Party Caucus. Akin also promised to restore faith in God as the center of public life in America and had consistently voted to defend the sanctity of human life. The other candidates' campaign themes were also fairly and fully described: Brunner was a job creator and an ex-marine, while Steelman was fighting to end the "status quo."

The sample of Republican voters was then polled again, and we saw that the candidates' messages drastically changed the complexion of the contest: Akin now came in at 38 percent and Brunner at 36, while Steelman was still at 15. Akin's narrative could make him the winner among the people most likely to vote in the Republican primary—and maybe, just maybe, a loser among moderate Missourians.

Tom Kiley, my pollster, turned up some findings that seemed crazy to me. For example, less than one quarter of the likely Republican primary voters believed that Barack Obama had been born in the United States. These were the voters who could help tip a Republican primary to an archconservative, but that conservative would have a hard time winning the state. Yes, it was a three-way primary of equally viable candidates, but a subset of energized people with strong religious convictions and serious aversion to gay people, public schools, immigrants, and reproductive choice could help elect someone like Akin. I began to consider whether it would be useful to help Akin spread his message, keeping in mind that he was the weakest fundraiser out of the three potential nominees.

Akin's track record made him my ideal opponent. Many of his votes in Congress contradicted his claim of being a fiscal conservative. While he opposed President Obama's authority to raise the debt limit, during the Bush administration, in 2004, he had voted to raise the limit by $800 billion. A vocal opponent of the Obama administration's stimulus efforts, in 2001 Akin had voted in favor of a $25 billion stimulus package that mostly benefited large corporations and the wealthy. And he was a big earmarker: in one fiscal year he sponsored or cosponsored $14 million worth of pork and once sought $3.3 million in a special appropriation for a highway near nine acres he owned and was planning to develop. While opposing spending money for child nutrition programs, veterans' health benefits, and disaster relief, he repeatedly voted to raise his own salary.

His extreme positions on social issues and ridiculous public statements made him anathema to many independent voters. He sponsored an amendment that would define life as beginning at conception, thereby outlawing common forms of birth control. He voted against repeal of the military's "don't ask, don't tell" legislation. When the Affordable Care Act was being debated, he stood on the House floor and asked for God's help in keeping the nation from "socialized medicine." In 2008, he claimed in a House floor speech that it was "common practice" for doctors to conduct abortions on women "who were not actually pregnant." He had made speeches calling for America to pull out of the United Nations and claiming the government had "a bunch of socialists in the Senate" and a "commie" in the White House.

So how could we maneuver Akin into the GOP driver's seat?

Using the guidance of my campaign staff and consultants, we came up with the idea for a "dog whistle" ad, a message that was pitched in such a way that it would be heard only by a certain group of people. I told my team we needed to put Akin's uber-conservative bona fides in an ad—and then, using reverse psychology, tell voters *not* to vote for him. And we needed to run the hell out of that ad.

My consultants put together a $1.7 million plan. Four weeks out we would begin with a television ad boosting Akin, which my campaign consultant Mike Muir dubbed "A Cup of Tea." We would spend $750,000 at first and run it for eight or nine days. Then we'd go back into the field and test to see if it was working. If it was, we'd dump in more "McCaskill for Senate" money, and we'd add radio and more TV in St. Louis and Kansas City. The second TV buy would approach $900,000. We hoped that some of our friends watching the TV ads would catch on and some of the outside groups would augment the last week with mail and radio. Sure enough, a radio ad calling Akin "too conservative" that went on the air in the closing days of the primary was paid for by the Democratic Senatorial Campaign Committee. We would later find out that their rural radio buy was $250,000.

The production costs for our television ad about Akin were pretty low, about $20,000, because we didn't have to film anything. We just used pictures and voice-overs. If we could see that the plan was moving Akin ahead, we would go for broke. As it turned out, we spent more money for Todd Akin in the last two weeks of the primary than he spent on his whole primary campaign.

If we were going to spend that kind of money on ads for Akin, I wanted to get him nominated and start disqualifying him with independent voters at the same time. By that prescription, our ad would have to include Akin's statement that Obama was a "menace to civilization" and that Akin had said of himself that he was "too conservative" for Missouri. This presentation made it look as though I was trying to disqualify him, though, as we know, when you call someone "too conservative" in a Republican primary, that's giving him or her a badge of honor. At the end of the ad, my voice was heard saying, "I'm Claire McCaskill, and I approve this message."

It started to work. Our telephones were ringing off the hook with people saying, "Just because she's telling me not to vote for him, I'm voting for him. That's the best ad for Akin I've ever seen!" A man wrote a letter to the editor of the *Springfield News Leader*: "I think it's time for someone who may be too conservative. Thank you, Senator McCaskill, for running that ad. You have helped me determine that my vote needs to go to Akin." The editorial page of the *St. Louis Post-Dispatch* advised those who were going to vote in the Republican primary to cast their ballot for Akin since he was "the most honest candidate. We suggest Mr. Akin because with him at least you're sure of what you're getting. He isn't faking it when he endorses the worst of the GOP agenda. He actually believes it. What you see is what you get."

A *Post-Dispatch* poll conducted July 23–25 showed Brunner leading the race at 33 percent, followed by Steelman at 27, and Akin at 17. But our polling showed the race was tightening, with Brunner still up by a point or two and Steelman solidly in third. Then, unexpectedly, the Akin camp took down one of his own ads that had been so effective. In it Mike Huckabee, the former governor of Arkansas and a leading voice in the conservative movement, endorsed Akin and explained his reasoning looking straight into the camera. It was powerful, but Akin's camp replaced it with Akin talking about "flames of freedom." What were they thinking? Akin didn't have money for polling, but we had been tracking the numbers carefully and concluded that he'd be in trouble if he didn't get the Huckabee ad back up.

On the Thursday before the election, I called Ron Gladney, the husband of Congresswoman Jo Ann Emerson, a Republican from Missouri. I asked him if he could get a message to the Akin camp to put the Huckabee ad back up. Of course Gladney started laughing and asked, "Are you kidding?" "No," I replied. "If he gets the Huckabee ad back up by Friday, he's going to win." I also placed a call to Michael Kelley, a Democratic Party and labor operative who was friends with a former Akin staffer, and asked him to convey the same message to the Akin camp. A short time later my campaign manager, Adrianne Marsh, got a call from the Akin campaign. The person on the line wanted to talk to our pollster. Adrianne called me, and I gave clearance, allowing Kiley to speak in broad generalities. Three hours later the Huckabee ad was back up.

This was the most fun I'd had in a long time. Akin had moved into a dead heat with Brunner.

I had a feeling it was going to work after my stepson and his family came over to our house after church on the Sunday before the primary election. He showed us what they'd found on their car's windshield after the services: a campaign folder containing information about Todd Akin, James Dobson and his Focus on the Family, as well as pictures of Todd and his wife, Lulli, on their wedding day. The brochure, aimed specifically at churchgoers, was entitled "The Story of a Sinner Saved by Grace." In it Akin described how he accepted Christ as his savior, gave up career ambitions as an engineer to attend seminary, and served on the board of Missouri Right to Life.

There was an issue on the ballot that promised to attract like-minded people to the polls: an amendment to the Missouri Constitution that expanded the existing right to worship God with a more explicit guarantee of public prayer and a new privilege allowing students to opt out of assignments that ran contrary to their religious beliefs. While not everyone in the Republican primary who voted for that amendment also voted for Akin, I believe the churches urging people to vote for the prayer amendment helped drive up voter turnout that naturally favored Akin.

I promised my two daughters, Lily and Maddie, that I would shotgun a beer if Akin won the primary. Although I had never shotgunned a beer in my life, I was more than ready for a celebration. That day—August 7, 2012—felt like my own election, even though I had no opponent in the Democratic primary. Never before had I been so engaged and so committed to another's race.

I decided to call it quits early. After leaving a room of enthusiastic volunteers north of the river in Kansas City, my daughters, Joseph, and I headed to the hotel suite where we planned to monitor the election results. We were in a car while most of the key staff followed in "Big Blue," the recreational vehicle we used for our mobile campaign headquarters. There was some nervous chatter as we pulled out of the parking lot, but I was pensive. I didn't feel like talking. I distinctly remember being surprised that my palms were sweaty. All of a sudden I understood the enormous risk I had taken:

I had spent millions trying to control the outcome of the Republican primary. If it worked, some would call it political genius; if it failed, and especially if I went on to lose in November, it would be called the stupidest thing I had ever done.

I was fully aware of the risk and would have felt terrible if Todd Akin had become a United States senator. On the other hand, if you went down the list of issues, there was not a dime's worth of difference among the three primary candidates on how they would have voted if they had become senators. Getting Todd Akin as the opponent in the long run made it more likely that Missourians would not be represented by someone who held those extreme views.

As the polls closed at seven o'clock, the mood seemed artificially festive. People were trying to joke around, but everyone was anxious. It was weird behavior for a campaign team awaiting the results of a primary election. Here I was in sloppy sweat pants, my top team members in jeans, everyone on cell phones, with a laptop on every lap and every surface. A lot of untouched beer and liquor sat on tables as we watched the clock, refreshed the page, and waited for the phone to ring.

Maddie and Lily understood the stakes. That's why all evening, as we waited for results, they were squeezing my hand or quietly sitting next to me, why, as I walked away from the buzzing expectation in the living room to find quiet in the adjoining bedroom, one or both would follow and give me a hug. Those moments were some of my best as a parent.

Akin ended up receiving 217,468 votes, compared to 180,821 for Brunner and 176,189 for Steelman. In the privacy of our suite, all I could do was celebrate privately and send an email to my team congratulating them on the work they had done.

After hugging my husband and calling my son in St. Louis, it was time for me to keep my promise. My daughters had to show me how to shotgun a beer. You punch a hole in the side of a beer can while holding it horizontally. Then you invert the can upside down over your mouth and pull the aluminum tab. Beer gushes into your mouth and you have to swallow quickly to avoid a big mess. I did it. And we laughed until we cried.

How much did "Operation Dog Whistle" contribute to Akin's victory? I do believe his nomination reaffirmed more than ever his conviction that a higher power had chosen him for this race. For Akin, government service is defined and guided by his religious faith. He was known to start committee meetings with prayers that included "in Jesus's name." He'd made religion a centerpiece of his campaign, saying his faith got him into politics and directed the things he did once in office. In my opinion his belief that he is a "holy warrior" doing battle with the forces of evil liberalism blinded him to the realities of political life and what might be best for his party. In the first lines of his election-night speech, he thanked God for hearing the prayers of his supporters and granting him victory. He probably didn't realize that we had also been praying for his victory.

While I got the opponent I wanted, polls showed I was still the underdog. But I knew Akin had said things that could disqualify him with a wide swath of Missouri voters. Just a year earlier he had said, "At the heart of liberalism really is a hatred for God." We knew we'd be able to use his own words to show that he was against Social Security, Medicare, and student loans. Right after the primary election, during a visit to the State Fair, Akin criticized the federal school lunch program. Then he was interviewed on a Kansas City radio station and said the morning-after pill should be illegal for rape victims.

Akin said so many controversial things that we began calling him "the gift that keeps on giving." Little did we know what he would say next.

CHAPTER TWELVE

The Magic Uterus

I begin with a confession. I did not watch Todd Akin's television interview that contained his explosive "legitimate rape" remark when it originally aired. That seems strange because that event changed so much so quickly. But the interview was broadcast on a Sunday morning, and that Sunday morning, like most, was a "grits morning" at our house in St. Louis.

My husband carries on a tradition that began with his father. He comes down to the kitchen early, takes the meat out of the fridge, and begins work on a huge pot of grits. One week he might use smoked sausage, the next week bacon, and some weeks he might use ham. The constant is the cheese. Usually all the kids come over, his and mine, and bring their wives, husbands, significant others, children, whoever is available. Since we have a blended family of seven children and eight grandchildren, it is always a big crowd of loving chaos.

As it was a grits morning, I didn't bother to watch Akin on Charles Jaco's interview program on August 19, 2012, when he made a statement that would rock the political world. Certainly my campaign staff and I knew the interview was coming. We were waiting for it, watching for it, but the heads-up we received didn't predict what was to come.

At 9:32 a.m. Cameron Sullivan, a tracker for my campaign, emailed a report on Akin's TV appearance. If today's campaigns demonstrate anything, it's that visuals make all the difference. You can *say* your opponent stands for a radical position, but it's much better to *show* your opponent voicing that position.

Cameron's tracker report was very comprehensive, including this sentence several paragraphs down: "Akin suggested that a woman who is 'legitimately raped' generally doesn't get pregnant because her body protects her. Akin said if she somehow did [get pregnant], we should punish the rapist and not the child."

After seeing the tracker report, I asked to see the actual video clip of what Akin said. My first reaction can be found in an email I sent at 11:22 that morning: "Jaw dropping." The email went to Adrianne Marsh, my campaign manager, and Caitlin Legacki, my communications director. "Need to light him up on this," I wrote. "Jaw dropping, that the body protects from pregnancy if you're raped!"

We didn't know it at the time, but an aggressive effort was already under way to rush Akin's outlandish statement into circulation. Cameron was not the only tracker watching his performance that morning. Bryan Finken, a St. Louis–based tracker for American Bridge 21st Century, was also poised to catch Akin's TV appearance. American Bridge is a Democratic Super PAC that grew out of the ashes of the 2010 election. With its opposition research and communications capabilities, a staff of sixty, and a two-year election-cycle budget of $15 million, the organization is primed to show Republicans for what they really are, using their own words and actions.

Federal election laws placed a barrier between my campaign and Super PACs like American Bridge. However, American Bridge and other Democratic-leaning Super PACs may coordinate their activities and share research and other information to eliminate duplication. I learned after the election that American Bridge had already created a three-hundred-page research book on Akin and passed it along to allies like EMILY's List, Planned Parenthood, and Majority PAC, in case they decided to run paid advertising.

Finken's briefing of Akin's remarks was emailed to the American Bridge "war room" in Washington at 9:54 a.m., Central Time. The video clip arrived within the hour. "As soon as we saw it, we said 'Go,'" recalled Rodell Mollineau, president of American Bridge. The Super PAC shared it with half a dozen allies, bloggers, and national news organizations. Talking Points Memo was the first to post it for the public to see, at 1:06 p.m. RH Reality Check, a weblog, put it out at 1:26. Soon Howard Wolfson, a Democratic political strategist, and Guy Cecil, executive director of the Democratic Senatorial Campaign Committee, were drawing attention to it on Twitter. Gawker posted it at 1:49, and Roll Call at 1:56. The slowest news day of the week in the slowest news month of the year had suddenly become very busy.

The broadcast of Todd Akin's interview on a sleepy Sunday in St. Louis was reverberating across the country and around the world like a sonic boom. Before sundown millions of people in the United States had learned what he said. And although he later apologized, suggesting he "misspoke" and used the wrong words, in fact what Akin said was articulated with authority and conviction. It was said in such a matter-of-fact way that either he had said it before or he had heard it before. Most important, he said it as though he believed it.

Jaco had asked Akin if his opposition to abortion included cases in which a woman had been raped. "It seems to me, first of all, from what I understand from doctors, that's really rare," Akin responded. "If it's a legitimate rape, the female body has ways to try to shut that whole thing down." Akin, a member of the House Committee on Science, Space and Technology, seems to have been relying on a discredited concept pushed by Dr. John Willke, an antiabortion activist and former president of National Right to Life.

If Todd Akin didn't know what he had done, his staff did. We heard later that, as they were leaving the television studio after participating in the interview, Akin's press aide, Ryan Hite, told him to never talk about women's bodies again.

Within a few hours of the broadcast, people with no prior interest in my race were logging on to my campaign website. My campaign team shifted into overdrive; we had to move quickly to exploit the opportunity Akin had given us. At two o'clock I put out a statement: "It is beyond comprehension that someone can be so ignorant about the emotional and physical trauma brought on by rape. The ideas that Todd Akin has expressed about the serious crime of rape and the impact on its victims are offensive." The statement went on to point out that Akin had cosponsored a bill to redefine rape and had opposed a state law against spousal rape because it might be used as a tool against husbands in a "messy divorce." References to medical studies showing that rapes do indeed sometimes result in pregnancies were included in the statement.

Shortly before 3 p.m. Alex Kellner, my campaign's digital director, dispatched an email to 150,000 people on our list with the subject line "You will be offended by this." The body of the email was this: "Are you sitting down? Todd Akin thinks that the female body can shut down pregnancy in the case of 'legitimate rape.' I wish I were making this up—read exactly what he said this morning." The message then quoted Akin's remarks word for word, adding, "It's not news that Akin thinks all abortion should be illegal—but his archaic, ill-informed justification is so incredibly offensive that

I had to share it with you." The message then asked for a campaign donation "so we can ensure that Missouri is represented by a senator who will fight for women's rights—not set them back fifty years."

By 6:30 that evening we had raised more than $33,000 online. The number grew to $45,000 in the next hour through the website and email. At 8:14 Alex reported that $57,000 had been raised, and at 9:10, $66,000. That evening John Coady, the campaign's finance director, announced that the income had boosted collections for the quarter to $1.4 million. From the emails and campaign ads, we acquired about thirty thousand more people for our email lists. People who had never donated to us before sent money, and people who had given money before were now donating multiple times.

Caitlin booked me to appear on *Morning Joe* for Monday morning, as well as NBC's *Today* show. The NBC segment was to be taped in St. Louis that Sunday night, and as my daughter Maddie and I drove to the studio, we were so worried that people would not fully understand how offensive Akin's statement was that we were saying it out loud over and over and over again. I wanted to make sure people actually heard the sentence. Little did I know how unnecessary that was going to be. Those words were destined to be repeated and replayed thousands of times over the following weeks.

Even by then the storyline had begun to shift. The discussion over what Akin said soon moved on to what effect it would have on his campaign. As his words were analyzed, the unfolding public conversation focused on how many others in his own party might hold similar views. This advanced to an examination into the collective mind-set of the GOP regarding women. Who else has Akin been associated with? Who else believes as he does? As the glare of the spotlight focused on Akin, the beam also fell on Congressman Paul Ryan, Republican Mitt Romney's vice presidential running mate.

At midafternoon Akin put out a written statement on his campaign website attempting to back off from what he had said:

"As a member of Congress, I believe that working to protect the most vulnerable in our society is one of my most important responsibilities, and that includes protecting both the unborn and victims of sexual assault. In reviewing my off-the-cuff remarks, it's clear that I misspoke in this interview, and it does not reflect the deep empathy I hold for the thousands of women who are raped and abused every year. Those who perpetrate these crimes are the lowest of the low in our society, and their victims will have no stronger advocate in the Senate to ensure they have the justice they deserve.

"I recognize that abortion, and particularly in the case of rape, is a very emotionally charged issue. But I believe deeply in the protection of all life and I do not believe that harming another innocent victim is the right course of action. I also recognize that there are those, who like my opponent, support abortion and I understand I may not have their support in this election."

The statement concluded by saying there were other issues to discuss, like the economy, the debt, and unemployment.

If Akin wanted to explain, clarify, retract, disavow, or apologize for the words he had said, this statement was about the lamest declaration he could have made. Its inadequacy became apparent the moment it was released on his Facebook page. Anger and cynicism exploded.

"I think everyone wants to know what you meant by 'legitimate rape.'"

"Making off the cuff remarks regarding rape shouldn't be made in the first place, and sir, you didn't misspeak, you meant what you said."

"Congressman, please bring forth the doctors and medical information that support these statements."

"What a fine, sincere expression of spin from your deeply empathic public relations staff."

"I did not see anywhere in this statement 1. an apology for your careless words nor 2. a recognition of the fact that the female body does not in fact 'shut that whole thing down' after being raped nor 3. an explanation of what you deem as 'legitimate' and 'illegitimate' rape."

It wasn't long before even conservative commentators began calling for him to get out of the race.

Perhaps no one was more interested in the possibility of Republicans capturing my seat than Roy Blunt, my Republican Senate colleague from Missouri. Despite the fact that he had been elected to the Senate just two years earlier, Blunt had already landed a spot on the GOP leadership team. That was based partly on his fourteen years in the U.S. House, where he had served in leadership positions. His standing in the Senate would grow considerably if he could pave the way for a Republican to beat me in Missouri, accompanied by the prospects of a GOP majority in the Senate.

I had known Roy Blunt for nearly three decades, since our days together in the state house. The political competition that had taken place between his family and mine was part of Missouri history. My mom had lost a state house race to Roy's father in 1978, and I had lost a race for governor against Roy's son, Matt, in 2004. Now, eight years later, Roy was working against me again, this time by helping Akin, his former House colleague.

Roy's worries about the Akin campaign's lack of professionalism and the candidate's unwillingness to take outside advice were realized that Sunday afternoon when his cell phone began buzzing. For the next seventy-two hours he would be on the phone a lot, trying to salvage the race for the Republican Party by trying to get Akin to withdraw.

I went to bed that night feeling optimistic, but a phone call from Adrianne right before I fell asleep set me on edge again. After we had discussed the amazing day and as I was hanging up, she said, "You know they will try to get him out." Todd Akin had exceeded even our expectations, but now there was danger that all of our effort was in jeopardy. We had worked to get him as my opponent; now we had to keep him there. If I had been a sorcerer's apprentice, it now seemed as though my political experiment was on the brink of going out of control.

CHAPTER THIRTEEN

Divine Intervention

The Monday that followed Akin's "legitimate rape" statement was the wildest day of my campaign. In all my years in politics, that day goes down as the most tense, the most stressful, and the most exciting. My on-the-road staff was made up of mostly young people, and in our four months together, traveling around the state, from the corn fields way north to the cotton fields way south, from the barbeque joints in downtown KC to the VFW halls in suburban St. Louis, we'd become our own little family, the "Road Warriors." I began to think they were getting the wrong impression of political campaigns. Not all campaigns were like this, a ride on a crazy roller coaster, I told them. One moment I would sing "Everybody Dance Now," and we would. The next, after reading a text or tweet that suggested Akin was going to drop out, it was like we were in the inside of a hearse.

Arriving at a veterans event in Festus early that afternoon, I met reporters posted like pickets at the entrance to the VFW hall. Responding to questions, I calmly sympathized with Akin for the first time, noted his apology that day on the *Huckabee* show, and made a point of mentioning that his party had nominated him. My political antenna is good, but that day it was on the fritz. I was panicked. Do I continue to criticize him, or, in an effort to keep him as the candidate, do I try to shore him up? Would that be phony? As I walked into the VFW hall, my mind was going a million miles an hour and my heart was in my throat. When I took questions from the audience—there were no questions from the small group of veterans about Akin—a man stood up and explained that he had lost 10 percent of his hearing in his right ear. He wanted to know whether I could get him any help through the Veterans Administration.

Of course I wanted to help him with his problem, but at that moment, with pressure building, I wanted to tell him I was in the middle of a national political crisis. I just couldn't deal with his problem at that particular moment. But instead I calmly explained the help my office could provide in straightening out his problem. This was the first of many times over the next weeks that Missourians made it clear they couldn't care less about the drama surrounding Todd Akin's candidacy. They wanted to know if I could help them get their veterans' benefits, keep their post office open, get drought relief to help feed their cattle.

For the rest of that tour, between stops I asked friends who had close Republican contacts to find out what was happening with Akin. If he withdrew, who would take his place? The names being discussed were Ann Wagner, the congressional candidate running for Akin's old seat, and U.S. Representative Jo Ann Emerson from southeast Missouri. Emerson was worrisome because she was a good campaigner, smart, and would have no trouble raising national money.

We learned later that on that Monday afternoon, Akin flew

to Ohio to meet with Rex Elsass, a national media strategist, who was trying to salvage his campaign. Elsass's firm, Strategy Group for Media, was one of the heavyweights in the business of Republican image enhancement. Clients included the Republican National Committee, the National Republican Senatorial Committee, and Citizens United PAC. Elsass produced the Akin apology ad, another attempt by the Republican candidate to claw back into the good graces of Missouri voters. The ad hit the airwaves the following day.

"Rape is an evil act," a contrite Akin said to the camera. "I used the wrong words in the wrong way. And for that, I apologize. As the father of two daughters, I want tough justice for predators, have a compassionate heart for the victims of sexual assault, and I pray for them. Fact is, rape could lead to pregnancy; the truth is rape has many victims. The mistake I made was in the words I said, not in the heart I hold. I ask for your forgiveness."

The apology ad did little to erase the impression that Akin had become a big liability to the cause of the Republican Party regaining the Senate. He highlighted an issue that displayed the stark differences between Mitt Romney and Barack Obama. The president wanted insurance companies to cover birth control; he wanted to preserve federal funding for Planned Parenthood; and he believed in protecting access to abortion. Romney said he'd outlaw abortion except in cases of rape, incest, and threat to the woman's life. The Obama campaign had been using people like Sandra Fluke, the Georgetown Law student pilloried by Rush Limbaugh for wanting birth control, as campaign surrogates.

I don't think the Republicans realized that they were telling women who seek contraception that they are less devout, less faithful to God. That idea is fundamentally insulting, and it encourages women to believe most men do not understand them. There are scenes that reinforce this conclusion. Take the House hearing in February 2012 on the issue of contraception and the Affordable Care Act. The photo of the all-male witness panel was widely circulated.

While men may not have noticed it, women who saw it felt *Isn't that just typical? These guys really don't get it.* Todd Akin personalized and crystallized all that and made women candidates the beneficiaries of the enthusiasm of women all across the country.

That Monday, armed with this ammunition, the Obama campaign had email messages and news releases ready to go, lambasting both Akin and the GOP platform. I called David Axelrod and David Plouffe on the Obama reelection campaign team and asked them to hold their fire, at least until after the deadline for Akin to get off the ballot, which was five o'clock on Tuesday. Axelrod stopped the news release from going out.

On the way back to St. Louis that night, after our last veterans event had concluded in Cape Girardeau, I reached out to Jo Ann Emerson. I told her I was hearing that she might wind up being my opponent. I wanted to hear from her that it wasn't true, I said, because she was my friend, and it would be terrible if we had to face each other in a bloody-knuckled political brawl. She said it was too early to tell, that she didn't know if Akin was getting out. I told her I didn't play "bean bag"; if she got into the race, even though she was my friend, the contest between us would be a shin-kicking affair.

My first focus that Tuesday morning, hours before Akins's withdrawal deadline, was the letter Blunt was preparing, urging Akin to drop out. He got every current and former Republican senator from Missouri to sign under his name: Kit Bond, Jim Talent, John Danforth, and John Ashcroft, the father of the right-wing evangelical Republican movement in Missouri. "We do not believe it serves the national interest for Congressman Todd Akin to stay in this race," the letter said. "The issues at stake are too big, and this election is simply too important. The right decision is to step aside." We heard that Ashcroft's name on the letter might have hit Akin harder than anything else.

Using the senators' letter, Romney issued his own statement: "Today, his fellow Missourians urged him to step aside, and I think he should accept their counsel and exit the Senate race." Even more Republicans joined in: Governor Scott Walker of Wisconsin and Senators Kay Bailey Hutchison of Texas, Richard Burr of North Carolina, and Kelly Ayotte of New Hampshire.

As the deadline approached, Akin was again scheduled to go on the *Huckabee* radio show, and I was beyond distracted wondering what he was going to do. I had a luncheon scheduled and was going to be at the campaign headquarters for "call time," the chore of calling donors for contributions. At midday we heard that Akin was about to go on the air. With the clock ticking, we thought, *Here comes the moment we've been waiting for*. Adrianne Marsh was frantically trying to get the *Huckabee* show to stream over her computer, but the damn computer wasn't working. She was shouting and "pulling her hair" and because her door was open everyone in the campaign headquarters heard her.

Then we heard a roar from the basement, where much of the staff was housed. And I knew that Akin had just announced he was staying in the race.

The onslaught of Republican power would have been enough to force many politicians into hiding. But not Todd Akin. I don't think any of those Republican big shots stopped to think about Akin's character and what drove him. I don't think they took into account how Akin would react to bullying. For one thing, he did not believe he owed the party establishment anything. No one in it had much loyalty to him, and the feeling was mutual. In Congress he was known as a loner, even among the members of his state delegation. No Republican official or operative had a close bond with him. His closest advisors were his son, Perry, his wife, Lulli, and God, in reverse order. He was accustomed to being down in the polls. He was used to not having money.

To help explain Akin's mind-set during this time, I turn to a conversation a mutual friend relayed to me. This friend told Akin he had to get out of the race for the good of his party, the country, and the principles in which he believed. Akin replied, "This race for me is God's plan." My friend responded, "But Todd, you won because Claire McCaskill helped you win."

"Sometimes God uses the devil in his plans," Akin said.

Meanwhile we were raising money like crazy off Akin's "legitimate rape" statement. In the six days following that broadcast, the campaign received over $1 million online. But the biggest dividend from Akin's remark was that we didn't have to convince people that he was an extremist. The first ad we used defined him with his own words: "On March 18th, 2011, Todd Akin said he didn't like Social Security. On September 3rd, 2011, Todd Akin said Medicare was unconstitutional. On March 16th, Akin said he wants to abolish the minimum wage. On April 21st, he said he would eliminate student loans. And on August 19th, Todd Akin said only some rapes are legitimate. What will he say next?"

On October 8 we began running ads in which rape victims talked to the camera. The ad with Diane was the most powerful. She's a pro-life Republican who said she had never voted for me before but would now because of Akin's position. She said she did not take the morning-after pill because of her faith, but she believed that if a woman is not given that choice, she is victimized all over again. The ad was strong, authentic, and powerful. We didn't run it a lot because we had learned from focus groups that people didn't have to see it more than once or twice for it to have an impact, and we ran it only at night because some parents were worried about having to explain the ad to their children.

Throughout the campaign I had been monitoring my mother's health. Wild horses couldn't keep her off the campaign trail during my previous election cycles. She loved it and was very good at it. But now I had to confront how ill she was. There had been medical episodes in the past, when there'd be a flare-up or a fall and she would be rushed to the hospital. But in the past she would bounce back, having good days when she wanted to go to an event or travel to a speech or just go to the nearby mall to strike up conversations with clerks and perfect strangers. "Are you voting for my daughter?" she would ask with a big grin on her face and a warm sparkle in her eye. Her mind was still sharp, and she asked pointed and insightful questions when I visited with her on my brief stops at home.

But that summer she no longer asked to go along, never insisted on a trip in the RV, and tired easily even when we were talking about her beloved politics. At eighty-four, her body seemed to be wearing out, and I couldn't bring myself to consider what it would be like without this woman of great intellect who had shared so much of her enormous strength with me. I was in close and frequent contact with my siblings, especially my older sister, Anne Moroh, who also lived in St. Louis. She and Sarah Dalton, who lived with our family as an assistant and caregiver, were monitoring Mom's condition while I was on the road.

After a long day of campaigning in late October, I was in Springfield in my hotel room when I got a call from Anne saying that she was on her way to the emergency room because Mom had taken a turn for the worse and an ambulance had taken her there. When Anne got to the hospital, I talked to her again and asked her to put the emergency room doctor on the telephone. "If it were your mother, would you come tonight?" I asked him. And he said, "I would."

I immediately suspended campaigning and in the dark of night rode home from the southwestern corner of the state, the car quiet, one of the staff driving and Maddie in the backseat. From Springfield to St. Louis, 215 miles, all thoughts of the campaign disappeared, and in the silence I reminisced about Mom. I thought about her teaching me how to sew. She would lay out a pattern on the dining room table and we would cut material to make a dress. All the while Mom would be on the telephone yelling at the governor or scolding the mayor.

I could still visualize her standing in the kitchen of my rental house in Kansas City many years later, when she and my disabled dad had moved in and Mom had gone to work as a financial advisor. I watched how at age fifty-four she learned that trade and worked on the telephone in my kitchen, night after night, making dozens of cold calls trying to close a sale. Prior to that, and for most of her life, Mom never got a paycheck for work she did outside the home. But she was a whirling dervish when I was growing up: PTA, the church choir, charities, Girl Scout leader, and politics. Always politics. I remembered a conversation that had taken place about eight months earlier. I was talking on the phone about my campaign with a man who lived in the Bootheel. He said, "Claire, you know it's going to be a rough one. President Obama is not that popular down here." After a long pause I asked, "Do you have any suggestions?" He did: "Are you going to campaign with your mom? She's a lot more popular than you are."

As I traveled the state, at every stop I made, people would ask me, "How's your mom?" When I came home from a day of campaigning, I would go up to her room at our house, and she would ask, "Are you going to rural Missouri enough?" I would tell her how often people asked about her. Mom loved Missouri, and Missouri loved her back.

We arrived at the hospital at three o'clock in the morning. For the rest of that week, my two sisters and I did twenty-four-hour shifts in her room. My brother came too, for part of the time. Mom got better for a few days; on Saturday they moved her out of ICU. But her condition did not improve. She hated the hospital, and it was clear that she was going to die, so on Sunday my sisters and my brother and I made the decision to make her comfortable at home with hospice. On the following day we took her home. About an hour after hospice left, when we were all with her, she took one big breath and was gone. We were glad that she was able to die at home, and we were glad that we were there.

Many people had witnessed my mother's outward brightness, but they hadn't seen her inner strength and beauty. To me she was the sun and moon and the stars. All my life Betty Anne McCaskill provided invaluable support and encouragement. I would not be who I am without her. From earliest childhood, she was my role model and hero. I suspended campaigning from the moment I talked to that ER doctor, until after her memorial service, the following week, which took place on the Sunday before the election.

Election day dawned gray and rainy in Missouri with the temperatures in the upper 40s. Early that day thousands of get-out-the-vote volunteers all over the state were busy knocking on doors, encouraging Democrats to get to the polls. By the afternoon it had cleared somewhat, and the sun came out. That morning I voted in Kirkwood, accompanied by Maddie, Lily, and Joseph. I got in a workout, washed my hair, and spent some time with my daughters, selecting the music that would be played at our election-night gathering. I tried not to watch the clock and tried not to be nervous.

As the results started to come in, we could tell quickly it was going to be a landslide. In Boone County, in the central part of the state, where I was expecting 53 percent of the vote, I was getting 60. That same trend began appearing all over the state. I was even winning in strong outstate Republican counties like Greene and St. Charles. And the Libertarian candidate, Jonathan Dine, was taking more votes than we expected. People who didn't want to vote for me and couldn't bring themselves to vote for Akin were going with Dine.

It wasn't long before I began getting congratulatory telephone calls from senators and politicians around the country. At about 9:25 p.m. I got a call from Todd Akin. He conceded the race and congratulated me. "God's blessings on you because you've got a bucketful of problems to solve," he said. I told him he was a principled man and

I thanked him for his years of public service. I asked him to tell Lulli and the rest of his family that I had a great deal of respect for him.

After the race was called, Joseph and I walked down the hall to the room where our children and siblings were waiting. There were tears and hugs, and as I left to greet my supporters, out of the corner of my eye, I saw the framed picture of my mom that someone had brought. Shortly after ten o'clock I walked out onto a stage with my husband and family to celebrate with the hundreds of supporters who had assembled in the hotel's ballroom. "Eighteen months ago there was a lot of the political chattering classes that were spouting a lot of information about the Senate race in Missouri," I said. "And they all said it's over. It's done. It's too red. It's just too red. There is no way Claire McCaskill can survive. Well you know what happened? You proved them wrong.

"There is one person missing off of this stage tonight, and I just got to tell you, 'Mom, this one's for you.' And the reason I know that this one is for my mom is because I actually believe when all of the votes are counted, something extraordinary will have happened. Because you need to understand that this race was called before any of the votes from St. Louis City or St. Louis County or Kansas City were counted. 'Guess what Mom? I think we finally won rural Missouri!'"

CHAPTER FOURTEEN

A New Civility

The "women senators only" bathroom near the Senate floor was very small and had just two stalls. On November 14, 2012, both stalls occupied, I stood waiting in the cramped bit of available space. The door to the hall opened and in came Senator Amy Klobuchar, a Democrat from Minnesota. Then the door opened again and the newly elected Deb Fischer, a Republican from Nebraska, whom I had never met, entered. An instant later the door opened for a third time; it was another new senator, Elizabeth Warren, a Democrat from Massachusetts. There we were, six of the now twenty women senators, jammed into the small bathroom designed for a Senate with only a handful of women.

"Too funny," I tweeted later, "first power meeting w/E. Warren and D. Fischer? In the 'Senators Only' women's bathroom. Gonna need a bigger bathroom."

When I first arrived in the Senate a historic number of women were serving: sixteen. That was the day I was stopped at the door of the Senate Chamber and was told there were no floor passes available for the swearing-in session that was about to occur. After I explained that I thought I had earned my floor pass by winning the election, the very embarrassed doorman apologized and fell all over himself trying to get the door open.

That incident reminded me of one thirty years earlier, when I first went shopping for office supplies in Jefferson City as a state representative. The store clerks said they could not approve the purchases until my boss called and signed off on them. I had to explain that *I* was the boss, an elected state representative. Some things have changed; some things haven't. Senator Klobuchar has recounted a similar story about her first day, when someone admonished her for being in the senators-only elevator.

To put things in perspective, only forty-six women have ever served in the Senate. New York's former senator Daniel Patrick Moynihan once called the place "a male preserve." Men not only ran the Senate but also held the key staff positions. Women performed clerical or administrative duties. How they looked meant more than their competence. Being the "good old boys' club" that it was, sometimes relationships between Senate members made a greater difference in what got done than the actual merit of an argument. Some rules were secret, and men made agreements during private social gatherings.

Until recent decades the majority of the women who served in the Senate were there as stand-ins or replacements for spouses who had passed away, some serving for as little as twenty-four hours or a matter of months, many only serving out their deceased husband's terms. Few were elected in their own right. During the two hundred years between the first Congress, in 1789, and the 101st, in 1989, only four women were elected to the Senate for full terms without succeeding husbands who had died in office. With the exception of

Margaret Chase Smith, a Republican from Maine in 1949, it wasn't until Nancy Landon Kassebaum, a Republican from Kansas in 1978, Paula Hawkins, a Republican from Florida in 1981, and Barbara Mikulski, a Democrat from Maryland in 1986, that women began making their marks as candidates elected in their own right.

When I arrived in the Senate, Barbara Mikulski was firmly established as the dean of the women senators, and she took her job very seriously. She reached out to each of us and spent time with us one on one. She wanted to make sure that we saw her as someone who could mentor and guide us. She is a terrific role model: tough as nails, no-nonsense, takes no prisoners, fights for what's right, stands up for herself. I have joked that there are very few people in the world I was afraid of, but I was pretty damn afraid of Barbara Mikulski. She's the one who guides us as we try to continue to set the standards for civility in the Senate today.

Barbara bears the scars of thriving in the Senate long before she had all of us for backup. When she first arrived in 1987, the only other woman there was Senator Kassebaum, with whom she served for ten years. During the time that Barbara and Nancy were the only women senators, it was Barbara who insisted on changes, such as getting us a gym and a bathroom right off the Senate floor. There was no place for women to exercise but multiple places for the male senators to work out. She fought those wars.

Like the bathroom, the gym that Barbara insisted on was a much smaller version of the gym for male senators next door. When my colleague Kay Hagan, a Democrat from North Carolina, was elected in 2008, two nice young men from the Rules Committee took her on a tour of the women's gym. As she looked around at the modest space and checked out the lockers and showers, she noticed the whiff of chlorine in the air. Seeing a door with a sign that said "Pool. Men Only," she gently asked the young men about the pool, and they informed her that it was small and "not very nice." She followed up after her visit, asking other senators about the men-only pool, and was informed that some of the male senators liked to swim in the buff, and that was the reason women were excluded. With her southern manners in place, she firmly and effectively informed the powers that be that even though it was a very small pool it still needed to be open to all senators. And so another gender barrier was broken, and swimming nude in the "men's pool" became another footnote for history.

In 1992, as civility on Capitol Hill deteriorated, Senator Mikulski began hosting dinners for female members as a way to build relationships. No staff is allowed. These dinners are primarily to support one another and to talk about whatever we feel like talking about. It is an opportunity for us to bond as friends. The sessions are also fun because you can let your guard down; once the doors close, everyone exhales. We all know that nothing that is said is going to be repeated or twisted or taken out of context. As Barbara says, "What happens at the salad bar stays at the salad bar." The relationships we have established have been incredibly important in helping us gain power in the Senate. Although we are far from monolithic in our political views, we support and protect one another, even when we disagree.

Our women senators' dinners are occasionally held in someone's home or off-site, but typically they take place in a room in the capitol, and they're modest affairs. There is no fancy menu and no long cocktail hour. They're a chance for us to talk about the issues of the day. It's in that room that we've agreed to work together on a number of issues, such as human trafficking and foreign adoption reform, and have forged some agreements on trying to avoid a government shutdown. It's where I struck up a friendship with Susan Collins, a Republican senator from Maine, with whom I've served on the Homeland Security and Government Affairs Committee. She had already done a great deal of work on government accountability and acquisitions, and I was very interested in getting at contracting issues in Iraq and throughout government. I found a kindred spirit in Susan Collins. She didn't think it was boring and wonky, as most of my colleagues did. Our ability to work together on these issues, combined with her independence as a moderate in her party, led to a trusting, close relationship. We've tried on many occasions to bring the two sides together. Susan will call me late at night and ask, "Do you think we can get a deal on this?" Or I'll find her in the hallway and suggest, "What if we tried this?" Her desire to forge those compromises is one of the things that makes her so valuable in the Senate.

The same was true of Senator Olympia Snowe, another Maine Republican. When I had some very lonely moments in my caucus, when I was swimming upstream and isolated from the majority of my Democratic colleagues, she sought me out and reassured me, telling me, "Be true to yourself, and it'll be fine." I miss her voice of compromise and moderation.

All the women in that room have taken difficult paths to get there. Even if you're from a bright blue state and you raised money like it's raining, campaigning still involves putting yourself forward in the most public way, to be inspected under the most detailed microscope imaginable. Male candidates aren't evaluated on their hairstyle or their choice of attire. Male candidates are not criticized for being too ambitious and too aggressive. Some people doubted our political ability simply because we are women. Even our own party leaders dismissed some women as inferior candidates, much like Missouri's Democratic Party bosses disregarded Harriett Woods in 1982. People like Mikulski and Patty Murray came up the hard way. Mikulski was a social worker who became involved in politics to fight a highway that threatened her neighborhood. Murray was a volunteer lobbyist fighting budget cuts. One thing we all share is the sense of comradeship that comes from knowing what we've gone through to achieve our office.

Spouses are not invited to our dinners. Every once in a while a child or grandchild might stop in to say hello, but even they are not allowed to remain for the dinner itself. But once a year we invite the women of the Supreme Court. Those dinner meetings are the ones I most enjoy, tales of which I will share with my children and grandchildren. It is heady stuff to sit in a room with all the women senators and Supreme Court justices.

I was over the moon when I had the opportunity to tell Justice Sandra Day O'Connor how meaningful her appointment to the Court was to me when I was a young assistant prosecutor. When she was appointed, there were no women judges in Jackson County and none on the Missouri Supreme Court nor any of the appellate courts. At that point in my career the only women I had ever seen in black robes were in a church choir. I also enjoyed getting a chance to visit with Justice Ruth Bader Ginsburg. In 1979, before she became a justice, she argued an important case before the U.S. Supreme Court, *Duren v. Missouri*, which challenged a state law that allowed women an automatic exemption from jury duty simply because they were women. Ginsburg and Lee Nation, a Kansas City public defender whom I knew well from trying cases against him, had argued that the law should be struck down because it devalued women's participation on jury panels. The Court overturned the Missouri law, which set aside a lot of verdicts. I was one of the young prosecutors who was tasked with going through all the files that had been overturned by this decision in order to determine how many of them we had to retry, whether we could get pleas on them, and whether any of them would have to be dismissed. That case was a huge event in my life at the time, and I was so gratified to have an opportunity to talk to Justice Ginsburg about it.

On the wall of my office is a photo of me with Justices Ginsburg and O'Connor (this was before the appointments of Elena Kagan and Sonia Sotomayor) and a framed copy of the original brief that Justice Ginsburg filed in *Duren v. Missouri*. Those are two mementoes from my time in the Senate that I'll always treasure.

A few of our dinners have been unsettling, due to a certain amount of cynicism that sometimes emerges. When I first got to the

Senate, the first bill we debated was an ethics measure that was a re-action to a number of scandals in Congress. The ethics bill contained a variety of reforms, including doing away with corporate jet travel for the Senate and redefining appropriate gifts. It also proposed ethics investigations and consideration of whether we would continue to have a bipartisan committee handling ethics complaints or would establish an independent office excluding senators. At an early women's dinner, I heard some express the fear that the office would create a "witch hunt" mentality among the media. I remember thinking to myself, *Well, that's different. I don't remember ever hearing women worrying about independent ethics investigations.* Although the level of "gotcha journalism" directed at the Senate was a far cry from what I had to worry about when I was state auditor in Missouri, some of my women colleagues had a jaundiced view of whether the media would handle these investigations in a responsible way.

In those early years the dinners were also an opportunity for me to spend time with Hillary Clinton. She not only came to the dinners but fully participated in the discussions and, despite having been the wife of a president, blended in seamlessly with the other women senators. She is a hard worker and highly respected because of it. She never played the diva card, never tried to separate herself as if she were different or better, though it would have been easy for her to do. She was the only one of us who had a Secret Service detail, the only one who had been first lady of the country, who had traveled to places with a much more rarefied atmosphere than even the U.S. Senate. But she never put on airs. She was kind and personable, and she was one of us. In spite of all the rhetoric you may hear the male senators too had respect for Hillary, regardless of their party or their political views.

The changes in the Senate since my first few years have been significant. Not only has the number of women senators increased, from sixteen to twenty, but in the process many have achieved the seniority necessary to obtain leadership positions. When I first arrived, it seemed to me that most of the women who were in leadership positions did not have enough power or enough authority to move the agenda or have a major influence on policy. Mary Landrieu of Louisiana chaired the Small Business Committee. California's Dianne Feinstein was chair of the Rules Committee, an important committee but not one at the center of power. Barbara Boxer was chair of Environment and Public Works. It too is an important committee, as it reauthorizes expenditures for water projects and surface transportation projects and oversees environmental issues that Barbara cares deeply about. However the all-important Appropriations Committee still had never had a woman chairman in the history of the Senate.

Fast-forward six years later, and you had Patty Murray chairing the Budget Committee; Debbie Stabenow of Michigan chairing the Agricultural Committee; and Mary Landrieu chairing the Energy Committee. Barbara Boxer remained chair of the Environment and Public Works Committee, and Maria Cantwell, a Democrat from Washington, chaired the Committee on Small Business and Entrepreneurship. Dianne Feinstein chaired the Intelligence Committee at a critical juncture in our country's history because of its oversight of our intelligence operations. And Barbara Mikulski chaired the most powerful committee in Congress, the Senate Appropriations Committee.

We had been struggling for years trying to get a budget done, and then Patty Murray became chair of the Budget Committee, and in relatively short order we finally had a budget that was agreed to by the House and Senate. The budget created a framework and a blueprint for a level of spending for two fiscal years. Shortly after that, Barbara Mikulski, who is under five feet tall, became a Titan, moving heaven and earth to get a $1.1 trillion appropriations bill through. We hadn't approved an appropriations bill in years!

We first passed the Farm Bill in the Senate in 2012, and again a year later, but that's as far as it went. There was nothing happening on the House side. Many people would have just given up and said, "Well, we'll just keep using the same framework for our farm programs that's in place now." But Debbie Stabenow knew that reforms were necessary, especially to get rid of wasteful spending. We were paying federal money to very wealthy mega-agricultural corporations, even when they were extremely profitable. We were paying them if they looked at us cross-eyed. We were paying them no matter what. She was determined to save $23 billion by getting rid of the direct payments program and transitioning over to a risk program. While it's still not perfect—I'm not a big fan of the way the crop insurance title is written in the bill that we passed—it's much better than what we had. Debbie was able to convince those in my caucus who wanted her to go further and those in the Republican Caucus who didn't want to go that far, that this bill was a place where they could meet in the middle. So after a couple years of haranguing, Debbie got the bill through. It was magnificent legislating on her part. Frankly, she should have gotten more credit for that then she did at the time.

Dianne Feinstein always leads with substance not politics. She is thoughtful about the legislation she puts her name on and about her responsibility as chair of the Intelligence Committee, and until March 11, 2014, when she made her speech on what the CIA had been up to, she had been a staunch defender of the intelligence community. Because of her unique position, she and her ranking member know more about what our intelligence community is doing than anyone outside the Oval Office. She is briefed; she understands the spying programs and has defended them. So when she made the decision to go public and call out the CIA, she knew what she was talking about. She accused the CIA of improperly searching computers that Senate Intelligence Committee staff members were using to review CIA documents about methods of torture and secret detention, a search that may have violated the U.S. Constitution's separation-of-powers principle.

After she spoke, Patrick Leahy of Vermont, the Senate Judiciary Committee chairman, said, "I've heard thousands of speeches on this floor. I cannot think of any speech by any member of either party as important as the one the senator from California just gave." Feinstein's accusations were later proven valid, and CIA Director John Brennan apologized to her and the committee staff.

As 2014 drew to a close, the Intelligence Committee led by Feinstein was ready to release its long awaited report on torture. There had been protracted negotiations with the CIA and the White House over redactions and content. And Dianne was torn. We went to dinner, just the two of us. She was facing enormous pressure not to release the report, being told that it would place American lives in danger and potentially cause deadly reactions from our enemies around the world. She also knew that the details of this long and involved investigation would never see the light of day if she did not release it before the Republicans assumed the majority in 2015. While she needed no additional strength or determination, I reminded her at our dinner that the values of our country were at stake in her decision. A report like this would never occur, much less become public in China, or Russia, or North Korea. Our democracy works only if our government is held accountable. A few days later, in another historic speech on the Senate floor, Dianne Feinstein released the report. It was a proud moment for our country and for women.

These four examples show how women moving into positions of power have led to changes in policy and progress in legislation. Women were also working behind the scenes to further these developments. We would not have reached a compromise on the budget impasse without the involvement of Susan Collins and Amy Klobuchar and many others. It should be noted that the night prior to that agreement, most of the Senate's women gathered for dinner in New

Hampshire senator Jeanne Shaheen's office, where there was a lot of talk about compromise.

The fact that women have brought about change for the better in the Senate was recognized in 2014, when Allegheny College awarded its annual Prize for Civility in Public Life to the Women of the Senate for helping to end the 2013 government shutdown and in doing so helping to show the way to a more civil climate in Washington. The extent of the collaboration among women is sometimes overstated, such as when a magazine declared, "Women are the only adults left in Washington." But I do believe women are willing to listen, to compromise, and to share the credit. For the most part, they won't let their egos get in the way of what they're trying to do. And I do think a relationship of trust has developed among the sixteen Democratic and four Republican women senators. All of those nights talking about our kids, laughing with one another, and, between mouthfuls of chicken salad, dealing with serious policy matters—I think they have paid off.

The midterm elections of 2014 brought significant changes to the power and roles of women in the Senate. In a brutal defeat, the Democrats lost the majority and with it many women lost their powerful chairmanships. While we added two new women, Republicans Joni Ernst from Iowa and Shelly Moore Capito from West Virginia, both Kay Hagan and Mary Landrieu were defeated. The 114th Congress still has twenty women senators, just fewer Democrats and more Republicans. While Susan Collins and Lisa Murkowski have chairmanships, men will once again retake the gavel on the Budget, Appropriations, Intelligence, Agriculture, Environment, and Small Business Committees.

The 2014 election also changed my role on committees. While I no longer have a gavel on oversight subcommittees, I am still able to force the federal government to be accountable through my seat as ranking minority member on the Permanent Subcommittee on Investigations. This is the most powerful oversight committee in the

Senate, and my chair is Senator Rob Portman of Ohio. I also serve as ranking member on the Committee on Aging, with my chair there being Susan Collins. Both of these senators have good credentials as bipartisan members, and I have worked closely with both of them during my time in the Senate.

From my position on the Committee on Homeland Security I am following up with legislation drafted after the hearing we held on police militarization in the fall of 2014. After the fatal shooting of Michael Brown by a Ferguson, Missouri, police officer, I witnessed both the good and bad of police departments being equipped with military-style equipment. In the initial days after the shooting, I watched, along with the rest of the world, as a strong military police presence threatened the ability of people to exercise their First Amendment rights in the streets of suburban St. Louis. However, a few days later, I witnessed an armored vehicle rescue highway patrol officers from a very dangerous setting after outsiders had come to St. Louis to foster a confrontation with the police. Our hearing in the fall of 2014 on the three different federal programs that provided military equipment to local police showed that there was no coordination, oversight or accountability in these programs. I am working to reform the situation.

CHAPTER FIFTEEN

"A Vastly Underreported Offense"

When I took my place on the Armed Services Committee there were only two other women members, Hillary Clinton and Susan Collins. For the first few years I did an awful lot of work on contracting oversight, trying to get at the abuses and fraud that had occurred in Iraq. I also turned my attention to the way the military dealt with sexual assault cases. I was surprised to learn that the military was not maintaining rape kit evidence longer than a year. I knew an awful lot about this because I had handled so many sex crime cases as a young assistant prosecutor. And I knew how important physical evidence was. I also understood that the statute of limitations was an enemy in these prosecutions because most perpetrators of sex crimes don't offend only once, but a number of times. The longer you can maintain evidence from one alleged assault, the more likely that evidence will be useful in later cases. And often it takes more than one victim coming forward in order for a victim to be willing to cooperate with the prosecution.

During a hearing of the Armed Services Committee on February 17, 2011, I raised this issue with two of our military leaders, Secretary of Defense Robert Gates and Admiral Michael G. Mullen, chairman of the Joint Chiefs of Staff. I pointed out that there were allegations that a woman had been raped by more than one member of a unit and that a video of this rape was making the rounds of that unit. In another case a woman who had been raped went to the chaplain, who told her that she needed to go to church more often. "The rape kits are only kept for one year," I said. "I can't think of a police department in the country that would only hold on to a rape kit for a year. I just think that we have got to look at this problem in a systemic way in terms of do these women have a safe place they can go, are we gathering the evidence quickly, do we have experts available in terms of prosecuting these cases."

Gates and Mullen agreed it was a serious problem and said they had zero tolerance for any kind of sexual assault. Gates said that efforts were under way to reduce the stigma associated with reporting a rape, that efforts were being made to increase the number of sexual assault investigators and prosecutors, and that there had been an expansion of the victim advocate program. He said that although commanders have the authority to move someone accused of rape out of a unit, away from the victim, he was worried that it hadn't happened as often as it should have. "There is no question there is more to do," he admitted. Mullen added, "This is a vastly underreported offense."

In fact, according to the Pentagon, of the twenty-six thousand estimated instances of unwanted sexual contact in the military in 2012, as many as twenty-two thousand were unreported by the victim. Victims do not want to come out of the shadows and talk publicly about the most painful, private, personal moment of their

life. They particularly don't want to come out of the shadows knowing that our Constitution guarantees the accused the right of confrontation, which means that an accuser who goes to court must confront her attacker, who will challenge her veracity and her credibility. No wonder sexual assault is the most underreported crime in America. In the military, victims' fears of professional and social retribution, stigmatization, and continued harassment are increased exponentially.

After the 2012 elections, rather than two women on the Armed Services Committee, there were seven, and we began looking more deeply at this issue after learning of several high-profile cases involving abuses by commanders.

The most notable was a rape case that occurred at the U.S. Air Force Base in Aviano, Italy, in which an officer raped a civilian contractor. She came forward and reported it. The officer was a pilot, Lieutenant Colonel James Wilkerson, who was found guilty by an all-male jury. But under the rules of the Uniform Code of Military Justice, Wilkerson's commander, Lieutenant General Craig Franklin, was able to set aside that conviction. Franklin said he had doubts about the victim's credibility and a hard time believing Wilkerson could have assaulted a woman since he was a good father and husband. Then another woman came forward and accused Wilkerson of committing adultery and fathering her child.

I confronted General James Mattis, the head of the U.S. Central Command, over this issue at an Armed Services Committee meeting. "Do you really think that after a jury has found someone guilty, and dismissed someone from the military for sexual assault, that one person, over the advice of their legal counselor, should be able to say, 'Never mind'?" I asked. "I question now . . . whether there is any chance where a woman who is sexually assaulted in that unit would ever say a word." The decision in the Wilkerson case gave me a new sense of urgency. I filed a bill that would curtail the authority of commanders to overturn such cases and would strengthen accountability under the military's code of justice. And I repeatedly asked the air force to remove Franklin from command, since any way you looked at it, victims could not feel completely comfortable reporting these crimes with him in charge.

A few days later I was on hand when the Senate Armed Services Subcommittee on Personnel called all the legal representatives of the military branches to a hearing to explain how sexual assault cases were handled. Senator Kirsten Gillibrand of New York, as the chair of the subcommittee, convened the hearing. It was the first comprehensive Senate examination of sexual assault in the military in nearly a decade. And for the first time in history, the majority of the members asking questions of the military lawyers were women.

In the wake of the Aviano case, also known as the Franklin case, Kirsten Gillibrand and I began working hand in hand, determined to make major changes in the way the military handles these cases. We agreed on dozens of major changes, including limiting the power of the commanders, giving victims more power, and giving victims their own counsel, and compiled a long list of reforms. But we had one disagreement. In the military the investigation of these cases is handled outside the chain of command, and at the conclusion of the investigation the military lawyers make a recommendation as to whether the case should go forward to the commander. The commander then makes the decision whether or not to try the case. After much studying, consultation, and thought, I concluded that victims would be better served by keeping the commanders in the process. Kirsten believed that they should be removed entirely, with military lawyers having unfettered discretion as to whether charges are brought.

As the number of women in the Senate grows, and with it their promotion to places of power, it is inevitable that at some point women will occupy leading positions at opposite ends of important policy questions. That's what happened in 2014 when Kirsten and I were at the forefront of contrasting views over a single aspect of how to deal with the terrible crime of sexual assault in the military. It is very unfortunate that our one difference over the commander's role in the prosecution of sexual assaults overshadowed all of our agreements on so many other important changes that were designed to bring protection, representation, and justice to military personnel victimized by sexual assault. But the news media, which had made much of how the Senate's women were "playing nice," swarmed all over the first apparent "rift" among us.

I don't know what steps Kirsten took to become fully informed on the issue of sexual assault in the military, but I know what I did. I spent time with the victim from Aviano. I spent time with the prosecutor from Aviano. I went to the Pentagon and spent hours with military prosecutors. I downloaded the Uniform Code of Military Justice on my iPad and began laboriously going through it, decoding the similarities to and differences from the criminal justice system that I'm familiar with. I met with Eugene R. Fidell, who teaches military justice at Yale Law School and was a go-to resource for Senator Gillibrand; he believes the military should not have any role in the criminal justice process of crimes committed in the context of military service. I spent time with victims advocates, victims organizations, and with many survivors, some of whom did not want to speak publicly because they disagreed very strongly with some of the victims organizations.

After looking at all the data, I was convinced that victims would not be well served by removing commanders entirely from this process. When I reached this conclusion, I knew it was going to be a tough sell. But I didn't anticipate how truly difficult it would become.

The media framed the issue as pitting victims against commanders, not which system would be better for victims. All of a sudden I found myself accused of not being on the side of victims. It took my breath away.

No one in the Senate had held hands with more victims in the courtroom than I had. No one had come close to the years of pros-ecutorial experience I'd had putting rapists in prison. The notion that I was going to be characterized as coddling commanders and fighting against victims was enough to make me physically ill.

We did the research: in over ninety cases in just two years, the prosecutors had recommended that the perpetrator not be charged, but the commanders had overruled them and insisted that the case move to trial. Over ninety victims would never have had their day in court if the Gillibrand proposal had been in place. That's what the statistics showed. In contrast, there were very few cases in which military prosecutors had urged commanders to prosecute and the commanders had refused. Our research also showed that removing commanders doesn't help prevent retaliation, and it doesn't increase the reporting of crimes.

But I was losing ground on the issue. A high-profile victim whose experience had been included in the film *Invisible War*, a documentary on violent sexual assault in the military, agreed with our position and wanted to come forward. She was going to do a press conference, but her husband called me late the night before and said she'd locked herself in the bathroom because she had been confronted by one of the victim organizations about her support of our provision. Advocates on the other side had told her that if she came forward she was an enemy to the cause of justice for victims. Because of that we cancelled the press conference.

The most bizarre part of this debate was when Senator Carl Levin of Michigan, Senator Jack Reed of Rhode Island, and I got called into Harry Reid's office, where he dropped a bombshell on us. As majority leader, he told us he was contemplating trying to use that power to allow a majority vote to adopt Gillibrand's amend-ment rather than requiring the sixty-vote margin that is ordinarily necessary. Of course we were very aggressive in pushing back. He was talking to the senior woman of his party on the Armed Services Committee, who had personally prosecuted hundreds of rape cases, to the Democratic chairman of the Armed Services Committee, and to the second ranking member of his own party on that committee, which had adopted an approach different from Gillibrand's. Senator Levin actually told him, "I don't think you know what you're talking about. I don't think you've spent enough time and I don't think you even understand this issue."

And Harry Reid looked at me and said, "But what about the women?" Stunned, I replied, "Harry, what am I? What am I? I think *I'm* a woman. You have a disagreement in your caucus. I've never seen you take sides when there's a disagreement in your caucus." He thought better of it and allowed the vote to proceed as it would have on any other matter in front of the Senate. After a months-long battle, we ultimately prevailed by five votes.

My Senate colleagues and I had proposed thirty-six amendments to the Uniform Code of Military Justice on sex crimes in the military, and thirty-five had become law. Commanders have been stripped of the ability to overturn convictions and will be held accountable under rigorous new standards. Commanders will be evaluated in the future based on what kind of climate exists under them in terms of sexual harassment and sexual assault. All victims who report a sexual assault will get their own independent lawyer to protect their rights and fight for their interests—a reform that has no parallel in the civilian justice system. Prosecutors in civilian criminal courts have a job of finding the truth and seeking justice, not representing individual victims. It is rare in the civilian criminal justice system for a victim to be represented by a lawyer. Civilian review is now required if a commander decides against prosecution of a sexual assault case when a prosecutor wants to go to trial. Dishonorable discharge is now a required minimum sentence for anyone convicted of a sexual assault. It is now a crime for any service member to retaliate against a victim who reports a sexual assault. The pretrial "Article 32" process, which came under scrutiny following a case at the U.S. Naval Academy, has been reformed to better protect victims. The Article 32 process was a weird conglomeration of a preliminary hearing, discovery deposition, and grand jury proceeding in which victims were often put through an almost abusive process. The statute of limitations in these cases has been eliminated, a particularly important development in a sustained battle against sexual assaults. The "good soldier" defense has been eliminated; that's a controversial procedure that allows members of the military to offer records of good conduct to prove their innocence. Another reform gives the victim the opportunity to decide whether to stay in the unit or insist that the perpetrator leave. The law gives the victim a formal voice in deciding whether the case is prosecuted in the civilian or the military system. And there is a requirement that all of these reforms are enforced at the military academies.

The list of reforms is remarkable, and frankly it would not have occurred if it were not for all of the women of the Senate who worked together to get it done. Yes, there were two women of the same party who had a strong and genuine difference on a policy question. It was an honest policy difference. I remain convinced with every bone in my body that what I did was best for victims. And I'm sure that Kirsten Gillibrand is just as convinced of the correctness of her position. When it was all over and the vote had occurred and she came up five votes short, we approached each other in the well of the Senate and shook hands and smiled. Senator Jay Rockefeller later pulled both of us aside and said, "I saw that. I'm not sure that would have happened after such a bruising battle if that fight had been between two men."

The good news is that since our reform efforts began the rate of sexual violence in the military has begun to decrease, while the number of victims willing to come forward and report these crimes has spiked. The comprehensive report prepared for the White House by the military in December 2014 contained the latest data and painted a picture of progress. The report showed that one in four victims is now coming forward, compared to one in ten just a few years ago.

Importantly, there was a 62 percent increase in the number of unrestricted reports since 2012. Unrestricted reports represent those victims who are willing to come out of the shadows and hold their perpetrators accountable. The report also showed that the incidence of sexual assault in the military was down by 27 percent. And maybe most importantly, in anonymous surveys of victims and dozens of focus groups with victims across the military, the overwhelming majority of them expressed confidence in the ability of commanders to face and control this problem. More than three fourths agreed that the unit commander supported them (82 percent), took steps to address their privacy and confidentiality (80 percent), treated them professionally (79 percent), and listened to them without judgment (78 percent). While there is still much work to be done, especially in the area of peer retaliation, our reforms are making a real difference.

CHAPTER SIXTEEN

Redefining "Ladylike"

Todd Akin made a number of outrageous statements on top of what he said about "legitimate rape." Shortly after we faced each other in a debate before the Missouri Press Association, he questioned my demeanor as a woman. Akin told a reporter for the Associated Press that I had been more "ladylike" when I ran six years earlier against Jim Talent. In contrast, I had been "very aggressive" with him in our debate. To emphasize his point he declared, "She came out swinging."

This was not the first time someone tried to rein in my behavior with the *L* word. When I was in the eighth grade, one of my teachers said, "Claire, you talk too much. You are too bossy. You come on too strong. Young men will never be interested in you. And besides, it's not ladylike." I'm sure she meant well, but *unladylike* is just another label used to stifle, limit, or marginalize women. As this book has recounted, political opponents, party spokespeople, and media surrogates have thrown a lot of rotten names at me over the years, from "whore" to "commie babe liberal." *Unladylike* is not in the same category, but it is insidious and a slyer way of attempting to keep a woman in her place.

There are plenty of examples of politically sexist speech that have been used to hold women back. Before she ever ran for office, Patty Murray was written off as a "mom in tennis shoes." She turned that around and used it as a theme for her campaign. When he was running for governor of Massachusetts in 2002, Mitt Romney thought his Democratic opponent, State Treasurer Shannon O'Brien, was being too aggressive in a debate. He called her performance "unbecoming." Would he have said that about a male opponent? Republican Kurt Bills, who ran against Amy Klobuchar in Minnesota in 2012, referred to her as "Miss Congeniality," and his campaign called her a "prom queen" and "Daddy's little girl."

A study of voter attitudes conducted in 2010 by Celinda Lake, a Democratic pollster, showed that calling female candidates sexist names significantly reduced their political standing. The use of pejorative terms like *ice queen* and *mean girl* actually had greater impact on a woman candidate than criticism based solely on her policy positions or past experience. The study came out the same year that an opponent of Senator Lisa Murkowski, a Republican from Alaska, sent out a message on Twitter calling her "a member of the world's oldest profession," and a talk-show host referred to Senator Mary Landrieu as a "high-class prostitute." The study found that female candidates lost twice as much support when an attack was laced with even mild sexist language. "Sexism against women in the media has become normalized and accepted in a way that [it] would not be if the comments were racist," said Jehmu Greene, president of the Women's Media Center. "It dramatically affects women candidates."

The study's findings led to the formation of Name It, Change

It, an organization devoted to wiping out "widespread sexism in the media." This group has called out "fashion police" reporters who pointed out that Janet Yellen, President Obama's nominee for the chair of the Federal Reserve, had worn the same outfit twice in one month, once for her nomination hearing and again for her nomination ceremony. Would such coverage have been applied to a man? The group has also gone after the Associated Press for focusing on the pink tennis shoes that state senator Wendy Davis wore while she filibustered in the Texas capitol against an abortion bill. And it called out an NPR story about Senator Kirsten Gillibrand, which reported that she had a "soft, girlie voice" and that she was "petite, blonde and perky."

When value judgments like these are applied to women in public office it complicates the already tricky set of circumstances these women face. On the one hand, they have to demonstrate leadership qualities like seriousness, command of a subject, confidence, and competitiveness. On the other hand, a woman cannot come on too strong. She must be tough but also communicate her ability to be caring. A woman cannot be cocky. She must be strong, but also vulnerable enough that people can relate to her. It's a tightrope.

But managing ambition and femininity is just one of many tightropes that women members of the U.S. Senate encounter, and they do it without a net. Many of the multitasking women in the Senate demonstrate their traditional leadership roles on the floor, in committee meetings, and in public appearances while privately fulfilling the requirements of wife, daughter, mother, and grandmother. Senator Klobuchar tells the story of how she promised her daughter that she would take her to Target to get a swimming suit for the end-of-year eighth-grade pool party. "But we were voting on a national security issue, so my husband took her instead," Amy recalled. "I was about to go onto the floor to vote, and she called me from the dressing room, crying: 'Dad doesn't understand the difference between a bikini and a tankini. They said we couldn't wear bikinis but we can wear tankinis.' I said, 'Get him on the phone right now.' So I have him on the phone, and I'm explaining the difference and why she could get a tankini. At that moment I literally ran right into Senator Lindsey Graham as he is leaving the floor. I thought at that moment, 'Okay, I'm not balancing everything that well.'"

Like working women everywhere, female senators must weigh the need to be on hand for their children's school ceremonies against nighttime fundraisers and other political demands. Some women have given their Senate staffs orders that they cannot be scheduled for night work more than two nights a week. Others sometimes bring their children to political events, trying to meet two needs at once. I have done that myself. I will never forget one Saturday morning when I had to go to a neighborhood meeting and cheerfully told Austin, who was probably seven, that he needed to get dressed because we were all going to a "party." This was not unusual since I often brought them along to various events. When I left the room I overheard him explaining to his sister, who was five, "Okay, Maddie, Mom says we are going to a party. But always ask if someone is going to give a speech. Because if someone gives a speech, it is no party."

As mothers we sometimes don't realize how much our children absorb. Senator Mary Landrieu has recounted a story to me about the time when she was taking her ten-year-old daughter to an activity one weekend and stopped for coffee near Washington. As they pulled into the parking lot, she saw Congressman Ed Markey getting out of his car to go into the coffee shop. Ed had been Mary's nemesis on a particular piece of legislation, and his opposition had frustrated her. As she greeted him in the parking lot she turned to introduce her daughter. "Mary Shannon, this is Congressman Ed Markey." Ed replied, "Mary Shannon, it is very nice to meet you." Without missing a beat, young Mary Shannon looked up and said, "I know who you are. You have been fighting my mom my whole life."

All of us who are moms and elected officials have had moments when the balancing act is so extreme that it becomes almost surreal. My colleague Kelly Ayotte had one of those moments while serving as attorney general of New Hampshire. At the time she was appointed to the job, she was six months pregnant with her daughter, Kate. In September 2007 she gave birth to her son, Jacob. Two months later she was home giving her infant son a bath when the phone rang. On the line were the governor and the colonel of the State Police. Kelly put them on the speakerphone and continued to bathe her child as they explained that a man had taken hostages in Hillary Clinton's campaign headquarters in Rochester, New Hampshire. The man claimed to have a bomb. She continued to bathe her child as she calmly received the briefing. They requested that she travel to Rochester to coordinate the law enforcement response. "As I am focusing on the information and grasping the emergency at hand, I wondered if they could hear my baby splashing," Kelly recalled. She hung up the phone, dried her son, dressed him, dressed herself in her professional clothes, called her husband, who rushed home to watch their children, and drove to Rochester, where state and local law enforcement did "an excellent job getting the hostages out, arresting the hostage taker, and diffusing a dangerous situation." Later that night Kelly met a grateful Hillary Clinton for the first time.

There is guilt. No matter how hard you try to balance, there is always a nagging sensation that you are not doing enough, that you are falling short as a mother. It is important to recognize that guilt and then put it in perspective. All working parents experience the feeling, and mothers probably dwell on it more than they should. Working fathers may not dwell on it enough. There are plenty of fathers in the U.S. Senate, but I'm confident they do not have the same parental expectations of themselves as their colleagues who are mothers.

Yes, the schedule for political campaigns and holding public office is demanding and unforgiving. And yes, there are times when you must miss events in your family life and it is heartbreaking. But there are positive aspects to the juxtaposition of political office and motherhood. Even though certain scheduling conflicts are unavoidable, there is also more flexibility than with a nine-to-five, Monday-through-Friday job. If I wanted to take two hours away from the office when I was the elected prosecutor to attend my son's school talent show, there was no one to tell me I couldn't. And while I have worked many more than forty hours a week throughout my career, many of those hours were in the evening or on weekends, and many of the events I had to attend were family-friendly and allowed me some unscheduled time with my children during the traditional workweek.

Young women often ask me if they can "have it all." Absolutely you can, but you can't do it all perfectly. You must keep your priorities straight and keep your guilt in perspective. I did sacrifice time with my friends for twenty years as I prioritized my family and my work. And I truly did not sweat the small stuff. Dust bunnies under the bed? To hell with them. Clothes not perfectly pressed for school? Forget about it. I recently asked my children what they remember from their childhood that would reflect on my shortcomings as a working mother. My daughter Lily said, "I remember that other kids had homemade sandwiches in their lunches and I had those pre-boxed, store-bought Lunchables." My heart sank as I asked her if that was traumatic for her. She hugged me and said, "No, Mom, I was cool. Everyone wanted to trade their sandwiches for my Lunchables." I'm not sure that was true or if my daughter was trying to ease my guilt, but I know I worked hard as a mother. No problem was too small for my undivided attention when my children called. And my scheduled time away from work was sacrosanct so that I could make important memories with my children. I tried very hard to be creative and spontaneous when looking for fun and educational opportunities for them.

Young women who are considering a political role shouldn't be held back by name-calling or by labels that attempt to demean them.

We must redefine the adjective *ladylike* to mean "speaking out, being strong, taking risks, taking charge, and changing the world."

I have witnessed a gradual change in how women candidates present themselves to the voters. In the past thirty years they have stopped trying not to publicize the fact that they are mothers and have stopped apologizing for being vulnerable. Motherhood and family have become assets that humanize a candidate, helping her to connect with voters, especially women. That was demonstrated to me when I ran for governor and many people thought I was an aggressive and slightly obnoxious know-it-all. People knew I was tough and knowledgeable, but they just weren't sure I was human. So when I ran for Senate the first time, I realized I had to show that I was also a wife and a mother who had the same hopes and fears about my children as every other mother in Missouri. Ironically women candidates have more success at the ballot box when they act slightly more "like a woman" and "less like a man." Everyone remembers the turning point in Hillary Clinton's campaign for president when tears came to her eyes after a woman in a coffee shop in New Hampshire asked her "How do you do it?" Hillary Clinton was really struggling, having gotten waxed by Obama in Iowa. But then she had a raw, personal, and vulnerable moment in front of the cameras, and you could almost feel her campaign gaining strength.

When I ran for reelection to the Senate I learned how obstacles could be turned into advantages, how remarks like those made by Todd Akin and Rush Limbaugh could backfire and be used against them, and to raise money for my own campaign. As women move into top leadership roles, including that of president of the United States, there will be fewer male politicians who are uncomfortable with strong and competitive female opponents. When that happens, sexism in the media will diminish. Future leaders, men and women, will be blessed with the right to display a mixture of the traditional cultural strengths of men (assertiveness and competitiveness) and women (caring and concern for others).

Some people might say the way I helped Todd Akin become the Republican U.S. Senate nominee was not "ladylike." But political candidates, especially women, have to be engaged and expect that there will be times when they may get their hands dirty. Sometimes politics is a tough, bare-knuckle business. In an era when anonymous donors contribute millions of dollars to defeat you by distorting your record, when your husband's business activities are fair game for falsehoods, and when the choice on the other side is far-right extremism, it's time to rip out every page of the political playbook, start over, and write some new plays yourself. A growing number of women have learned this. Being politically strategic and taking risks must be part of every woman candidate's skill set. I have no regrets. Would Todd Akin have made as big an issue out of sexual assault in the military as I did? I don't think so.

Now I'm working with Senator Gillibrand and others to go after the silent epidemic of sexual assault on college campuses. And predictably, my work against wasteful government remains the meat and potatoes of my job in the Senate. In perhaps the biggest fraud in U.S. Army history, up to $100 million was wasted in a National Guard recruiting scheme that paid guard members, retirees, and civilians to recruit enlistees. The Guard spent more than $56 million on sports marketing with NASCAR to attract recruits and couldn't produce a single new soldier from the program. Almost $3 million in bonuses were paid to 2,800 federal employees with conduct violations, including more than $1 million to 1,100 IRS employees who were delinquent on their taxes. The agenda of our problems is a long one. But you can't use your clout to tackle the issues you believe are important unless you have the clout in the first place.

I want my story to inspire other women, just as other women have inspired me. There were so many women pioneers in my life, the first being my mother, Betty Anne McCaskill. She gave me the confidence and ambition to defy people like the guy whose door I knocked on during my first campaign, the one who told me to go find a husband, that I wasn't tough enough for politics. I think I've proved him wrong. I hope my story will help women get comfortable with the rough and ugly side of modern political campaigns, that it will encourage them to fight in the no-holds-barred races that will give them their fair share of power in our democracy.

For women to be successful in politics or the business world or any other endeavor, they have to be hyperprepared. I was marginalized as a young state legislator until I demonstrated a breadth and depth of knowledge about criminal law. I went from being the object of sexist jokes to being asked for advice and assistance on pieces of legislation. But I also rely on the lessons I learned during my waitressing days: Keep calm. Don't raise your voice. Be a good listener. Live in the moment. Give people respect. You may be tired and stressed, but keep a smile on your face as if you're having the best time in your life. And don't sweat the small stuff, or, as Aunt Beppy would say, "Don't perspire."

Stay grounded and don't take yourself too seriously. The "gosh aren't I important" mentality is a recipe for disaster. Children really help with this. My colleague Heidi Heitkamp has told me the story of a day when she was attorney general of North Dakota and had back-to-back meetings that she could not miss. Her eight-year-old daughter woke up that morning with a fever and tummy ache. Her husband was already off to work, she had no day care lined up, and people had already traveled great distances for her morning meetings. So she gathered up her sick daughter and a blanket and teddy bear and went to work. Her daughter rested quietly on the office couch while Heidi had her meetings and worked to clear her afternoon schedule. In the car headed for home, her daughter asked, "So, why do all those people think *you* can solve their problems?" Keeping perspective and not getting a big head is crucial, and nothing grounds a woman more than the innocent comeuppance delivered by her children.

On the other hand, don't be afraid to offend. Many women have the disease to appease, but you have to be willing to offend in order to make any progress. You have to be willing to offend to move policy in a way that gets things done. You can't be a leader without making someone mad.

Embrace mistakes. If you are wrong, say so. If you lose, learn from it. A setback may be the best gift you can get. If you're cast in the role of the underdog, use it as an excuse to take a risk. It is difficult to be a leader and a victim at the same time. While showing vulnerability makes you relatable and authentic, focusing on your vulnerability saps your strength. Don't be hypercritical of other women. Sometimes we are downright mean girls, criticizing women for behavior we silently accept when we see it in men. For a weekend date in the 1980s, when I was a young state representative, I put on a fuzzy sweater and a leather skirt that hit me just slightly above the knee. After dinner we stopped by a party where I knew the host. The next morning the host called me and said, "Claire, I've got to tell you this story about when you and your date arrived at the party last night. You walked in the door and this woman who was sitting next to me said, 'Who in the world is that?' I got the sense she was talking about you, so I turned to her and I said, 'That's a state representative.' And she said, 'Well, I don't care, he didn't have to bring a tramp with him.'" Don't be hard on other women. Reach out to them and mentor and encourage them.

Be authentic. The worst advice I've ever received was *Change who you are, how you look, how you talk*. In my very first campaign I had a head of long curly blonde hair. I will never forget a well-meaning older woman at one of my campaign events coming up to me and saying, "You are bright and articulate but you're going to have to do something about that hair." I ignored her and everyone else who has tried to "remake" me.

There is one other issue we all need to work on. While women do make great candidates, we still have progress to make as donors and fundraisers. As young women we are socialized to care about our security, but our idea of security is different from a man's. We see security as saving money for college, or putting money in a savings account, or finding a good bargain. Too often women don't see that they will become more secure by giving a financial contribution to a political candidate who shares their values and pushes for change they believe in. Women have to realize that the only true path to security in this great nation is through power. It is through power that we will be able to provide safe and affordable day care, achieve equal pay for equal work, provide preventive health care, make contraception available and affordable, and make sure we have a secure retirement.

For the past thirty years I have asked women I meet to take the price of that bad blouse in the closet and write a check to a candidate they believe in. You know that blouse. It was a really good deal. You didn't have time to try it on, but you liked the color. And it was such a bargain. You snapped up that blouse, brought it home, and when you put it on it gapped. Or maybe it wasn't the right color. So it hung in your closet until you finally put it in a garage sale or gave it to Goodwill. I still get checks from women who have written "blouse" in the memo line, proof that we are making real and significant progress.

The one moment that still motivates me was that day campaigning door-to-door for my first state house race in 1982, when the man slammed the door in my face. I tell young people to find their own slammed door that will push them to achieve great things. And while you're at it, knock on some doors to help elect other women.

Acknowledgments

My first thanks must go to Terry Ganey. He was my partner in this effort. He is a gifted writer and provided much needed structure and discipline to this process. Terry is a highly respected journalist who covered me for years in Missouri, and I always appreciated his doggedness in pursuing even the most elusive story that he thought was important. Now he is my friend.

Next I must express gratitude to my best friend and biggest supporter, my husband Joseph Shepard. He nudged me forward on this book, and as usual, he was right. Joseph has put up with a lot of nonsense because of my career, but always manages a smile of encouragement and boundless love.

My children Austin, Maddie, and Lily, deserve thanks for understanding their mom so well and being the kind of children who make me cry with pride.

My siblings, Anne, Lisa, and Will, have been my rock and a constant reminder that there is no more powerful force in the world than a united family. In fact all of my family, including my stepchildren and my nine and counting grandchildren, are a constant reminder of things way more important than elections.

A special thank you to Priscilla Painton, my editor at Simon & Schuster. Her enthusiasm for this book was contagious and gave me needed confidence. And her editing made it a much better "page turner." And a hug to my book agent, Amy Berkower, who morphed from my political supporter to my fierce advocate as we worked to get this book published.

And finally my respect, gratitude, and admiration goes to my staff of today and yesterday. For thirty years I have been incredibly fortunate to have the best and the brightest willing to work with me in the public sector. All of them are responsible for my successes. We have laughed, cried, worried, and celebrated together. I get the attention; they deserve the credit.

Notes

CHAPTER ONE

6   "We'd walk into a party": Joe Popper, "Blonde Ambition: State Rep. Claire McCaskill Is the Kind of Woman Who Knows Exactly What She Wants—Everything," *Kansas City Star*, Nov. 22, 1987.

6   "Despite her ambition": Ibid.

9   "She won everything": Interview, Betty Anne McCaskill, Feb. 17, 2011.

14   "It's really a very difficult crime": Terrence Thompson, "Arson Pays? Not against This Prosecutor," *Kansas City Star*, Apr. 22, 1981.

14   "She taught me how to use": Interview, Louis C. Accurso, June 9, 2011.

14   "She's not the least bit afraid": Popper, "Blonde Ambition."

CHAPTER TWO

22   "The Harlins were very active Republicans": Interview, Betty Anne McCaskill, Feb. 12, 2011.

22   Tan Harlin, on the other hand: *West Plains Gazette*, Fall 1980, 29.

22   "My mother had it hard": Interview, Betty Anne McCaskill.

24   "He was one of the ones": Ibid.

24   Twelve days after Harry Truman gave: *Lebanon Daily Record*, June 21, 1950.

25   "I just liked the excitement": Interview, Betty Anne McCaskill.

25   "There were six people in Texas County": Ibid.

26   "The sale was terribly hard": Ibid.

26   "If Uncle Tom didn't have that drugstore": Ibid.

28   "It is the considered judgment": Letter from Paul E. Williams to Jim Dalton, Division of Insurance, Apr. 4, 1969, Hearnes Papers, Missouri State Archives.

29   "An investigator is one of our most direct contacts": Letter from William McCaskill to Warren Hearnes, June 23, 1969, Hearnes Papers, Missouri State Archives.

29   "we have our heads in the sand": Letter from William McCaskill to Warren Hearnes, Dec. 17, 1971, Hearnes Papers, Missouri State Archives.

29   "I would strongly recommend you to contact": Letter from William McCaskill to Paul Polette, Jan. 8, 1970, Hearnes Papers, Missouri State Archives.

30   "The time has long passed": Letter from William McCaskill to Warren Hearnes, Sept. 4, 1969, Hearnes Papers, Missouri State Archives.

30   "Betty Anne is busy remembering": Letter, Christmas 1962, in possession of Anne Moroh.

30   "It started when I was too young": Lisa Finn's remarks at Betty Anne McCaskill memorial ceremony, Nov. 4, 2012.

31   "I consider myself a liberated woman": *Columbia Missourian*, Jan. 14, 1972.

31   "It wasn't just say your prayer": Interview, Betty Anne McCaskill, Jan. 3, 2007.

31 "I just decided I would emphasize": Ibid.

32 she proceeded to heckle her colleagues: *Columbia Daily Tribune*, Aug. 8, 1972.

CHAPTER THREE

35 "I'd made all those speeches": Patricia Sullivan, "Harriet Woods: Inspired Creation of EMILY's List," *Washington Post*, Feb. 10, 2007.

35 "It wasn't quite as serious": Interview, Harry Hill, Mar. 7, 2011.

36 "I felt like there were a few talented people": Interview, Doug Harpool, Apr. 28, 2012.

36 "There was a large freshman class": Interview, Vernon Scoville, Aug. 29, 2011.

36 "flowing blonde mane": Interview, Gracia Backer, Aug. 10, 2011.

36 "an electrified look": Interview, Harry Hill.

38 "After a while, I began to sense": Interview, Doug Harpool.

40 "In the Ozarks we would say": Ibid.

40 "We just didn't see eye to eye": Interview, Harry Hill.

41 "When we would go to parties": Ibid.

41 "These guys would always joke": Interview, Doug Harpool.

41 "[Claire would] walk by on the floor": Ibid.

42 "He was back behind us": Interview, Gracia Backer.

44 "Senator Webster had respect": Terry Ganey, "The Rise and Fall of Bill Webster's Golden Career; Son of Powerful Father Had It All," *St. Louis Post-Dispatch*, June 6, 1993.

44 "The legislature is a computer game": Roy Malone, "Carthage's Dick Webster: A Power in the State Senate," *St. Louis Post-Dispatch*, Apr. 20, 1982.

50 "Veterans of the General Assembly": "Missouri Legislator Expecting a Baby," *Kansas City Star*, Jan. 29, 1987.

51 "This is the most special guest": Steve Kraske, "Raising Austin," *Kansas City Star*, Jan. 10, 1988.

52 "a cruel and baseless insult": "McCaskill Accuses Senator of Insulting Her Character," *Kansas City Star*, May 1, 1988.

CHAPTER FOUR

60 "We had to portray": Interview, Steve Glorioso, Feb. 10, 2011.

68 "Spouses deceive spouses": "McCaskill Emerges as a Survivor: Prosecutor Weathers Events That Might Have Ruined Another's Career," *Kansas City Star*, Aug. 14, 1994.

69 "I want to congratulate you": Ibid.

CHAPTER FIVE

78 as one newspaper reporter quipped: Virginia Young, "McCaskill Touts Experience, Rural Roots," *St. Louis Post-Dispatch*, Oct. 24, 2004.

84 "a rip-roaring speech": Jo Mannies, "McCaskill Exudes Tough, but She's Not Running for Governor—Yet," *St. Louis Post-Dispatch*, March 28, 1999.

84 "McCaskill's hard-hitting performance": Ibid.

84 "McCaskill Soils Herself for Bob Holden": "Remarks Ignite Political Outrage—Democrat Suggests Firing GOP Official," *Kansas City Star*, Sept. 27, 2000.

85 "a new low in political rhetoric": Eric Stern, "Democratic Women Chastise Republican Spokesman; Secretary of State Urges GOP to Fire him for Comment; He says he Apologized to McCaskill," *St. Louis Post-Dispatch*, Sept. 28, 2000.

85 "It's pretty much the lowest thing": Ibid.

86 "The sexualized smearing": Rhonda Chriss Lokeman, "Always

a Volatile Mix: Politics and 'Hookers,'" *Kansas City Star*, Oct. 1, 2000.

86 "I couldn't believe Duwe": Rich Hood, "Sometimes in Politics You Can Be Right and Wrong at the Same Time," *Kansas City Star*, Oct 1, 2000.

86 "totally insensitive and wrong": Jo Mannies, "Busy Week in Politics Ignites Unrest Within Both Parties," *St. Louis Post-Dispatch*, Oct. 1, 2000.

86 "You don't see guys": Bill McClellan, "Talent Could Do without the 'Help' of GOP Spokesman," *St. Louis Post-Dispatch*, Sept. 29, 2000.

88 "It's a proper way": Terry Ganey, "It's Jean Carnahan vs. John Ashcroft: Carnahan Says She Would Fight for Late Husband's Values; She Serves If Mel Carnahan Wins," *St. Louis Post-Dispatch*, Oct. 31, 2000.

90 "It just worked": Interview, Joseph Shepard, April 2, 2012.

91 "It's harder to paint": Virginia Young, "Marriage Won't Halt Reform Effort, McCaskill Vows—Auditor Plans to Marry Nursing Home Owner," *St. Louis Post-Dispatch*, Feb. 11, 2002.

CHAPTER SIX

94 "a truly jet-setting pace": David Lieb, "Holden Is Frequent Flier on State Jet," Associated Press, June 24, 2001.

96 "I stayed with Holden": Interview, James B. Nutter Sr., Feb. 10, 2011.

98 "It is not an easy decision": Associated Press, "Woods Endorses McCaskill in Primary," *St. Louis Post-Dispatch*, June 24, 2004.

99 "When the Carpenters Union supports": Deb Peterson, "McCaskill, Holden Lock Up Support from Two Big Unions," *St. Louis Post-Dispatch*, Feb. 13, 2004.

102 "A male politician's wife": Interview, Joseph Shepard.

105 "Democratic voters were so divided": Ann Wagner, "Democrats Opt for More of the Same, Republicans Offer Real Change with Matt Blunt," Missouri Republican Party news release, Aug. 3, 2004.

105 "I just got requests": Email from Amanda St. Amand to Terry Ganey, July 16, 2004.

CHAPTER SEVEN

116 "When we flew out to Washington": Interview, Joseph Shepard.

121 "I call this the dog-and-pony show": Jo Mannies, "McCaskill Is Taking Race to Rural Voters: Democrat Believes She Can Win Them Over in Her Campaign for Senate," *St. Louis Post-Dispatch*, Apr. 16, 2006.

122 "She's the kind of woman": Jeffrey Goldberg, "Central Casting: The Democrats Think about Who Can Win in the Midterms—and in 2008," *New Yorker*, May 29, 2006.

124 "The Democratic Party has to look at candidates": Ibid.

127 "I haven't seen people want to touch": John Heilemann and Mark Halperin, *Game Change* (HarperCollins, 2010), 61.

128 "He has told the story": Interview, Joseph Shepard.

128 "She didn't run as a woman candidate": Terry Ganey, "Mission Accomplished: Claire McCaskill Chases Her Dream in Washington," *Columbia Daily Tribune*, Jan. 7, 2007.

129 "I voted for Claire McCaskill": Terry Ganey, "McCaskill Ekes Out a Win: Voter Angst, Campaigning Key in Victory," *Columbia Daily Tribune*, Nov. 8, 2006.

CHAPTER EIGHT

134 the "most egregious and blatant": Rudi Keller, "Farewell to Bond," *Columbia Daily Tribune*, Dec. 19, 2010.

135 "He kept going on and on": Interview, Adrianne Marsh, Feb. 7, 2012.

136 "In a caucus lunch": Interview, Senator Chuck Schumer, June 5, 2012.

137 the *Washington Post* published the work: Dana Priest and Anne Hull, "Soldiers Face Neglect, Frustration at Army's Top Medical Facility," *Washington Post*, Feb. 18, 2007.

142 "There is a special place": Al Kamen, "Run of President of Afghanistan? Zalmay, Zalmay Not," *Washington Post*, Jan. 9, 2008. Albright, a supporter of Hillary Clinton's candidacy, first made the statement in a speech in 2006 at a WNBA-sponsored luncheon in New York. Her remark later appeared on Starbuck's coffee cups that featured the sayings of prominent people.

CHAPTER NINE

148 there were more Defense Department contract workers: "Department of Defense Contractors in Afghanistan and Iraq: Background and Analysis," Congressional Research Service, May 13, 2011.

148 The air force paid a Florida company: "$600 Million Spent on Cancelled Contracts. Report: Work in Iraq Shoddy, Mismanaged," *USA Today*, Nov. 18, 2008.

149 monogramming hand towels: Associated Press, "Military Criticized in Report on Soldier Electrocuted in Iraq," *New York Times*, July 27, 2009.

149 faulty wiring in showers: Robin Acton, "Contractor KBR Given

$83 Million Bonus for Iraq Electrical Work," *Pittsburgh Tribune Review*, May 21, 2009.

149 ITT Federal Services International: Associated Press, "Defense Contractor Got $$ to Fix Shoddy Work," *Deseret Morning News*, Jan. 24, 2008.

150 One was retired marine general: Josh Boak, "Embattled IG for Afghan War to Testify," *Washington Post,* Nov. 18, 2010.

150 Mark Benjamin, an investigative reporter: Mark Benjamin, "Grave Offenses at Arlington National Cemetery, a criminal investigation and allegations of misplaced bodies and shoddy care have roiled the famous burial ground," Salon.com, July 16, 2009, accessed at http://www.salon.com/2009/07/16/arlington_national_cemetery/.

CHAPTER ELEVEN

170 "who were not actually pregnant": Nicholas J.C. Pistor, Kevin McDermott and Virginia Young, "Political Fix," *St. Louis Post-Dispatch*, Oct. 4, 2012. C-Span recorded the speech on Jan. 22, 2008.

170 "a bunch of socialists in the Senate": Alex Kane, "Akin's 10 Weirdest Moments, his 'legitimate rape' remark gets the most press but the GOP candidate has a trove of wacky thoughts and theories," AlterNet and Salon.com, Oct. 26, 2012 at http://www.salon.com/2012/10/26/ten_weirdest_things_akin_has_said/.

171 "I think it's time for someone": Scott Watson, letter to the editor, *Springfield News Leader*, Aug. 1, 2012.

171 he was "the most honest candidate": "Akin, Randles Win Credibility Test: GOP Primaries Are a Lesson in Stubborn Demagoguery," *St. Louis Post-Dispatch*, July 28, 2012.

175 "At the heart of liberalism": "Clergy Dissatisfied with Akin Apology," *Columbia Daily Tribune*, June 29, 2011.

CHAPTER TWELVE

177 The title of this chapter comes from Susan Campbell, "The Tale of a Missouri Republican and the Magic Uterus," *New Haven (CT) Register*, August 20, 2012, online.

178 "Akin suggested that a woman": Email from Cameron Sullivan to Adrianne Marsh and McCaskill campaign team, Aug. 19, 2012.

179 "As soon as we saw it": Interview, Rodell Mollineau, Dec. 6, 2012.

180 "It seems to me, first of all": "Jaco Report: Full Interview with Todd Akin," Fox2Now, posted Aug. 19, 2012, online.

CHAPTER THIRTEEN

187 "Rape is an evil act": Tom Cohen, "Akin Defies Mounting Calls to Withdraw from Senate Race," *CNN*, Aug. 21, 2012.

188 "We do not believe it serves the national interest": Ibid.

188 "Today, his fellow Missourians": Ben Schreckinger, "Romney Calls for Akin's Exit from Senate Race," *National Journal*, Aug. 21, 2012.

CHAPTER FOURTEEN

204 "I've heard thousands of speeches": Mark Mazzetti and Jonathan Weisman, "Conflict Erupts in Public Rebuke on CIA Inquiry," *New York Times*, Mar. 11, 2014.

205 "Women are the only adults left": Jay Newton-Small, "Women Are the Only Adults Left in Washington," *Time*, October 16, 2013, online.

CHAPTER FIFTEEN

208 of the twenty-six thousand estimated instances: Paul D. Shinkman, "Military Sexual Assaults Skyrocket as Hagel Announces New Plan of Attack," *U.S. News and World Report*, May 7, 2013, online.

CHAPTER SIXTEEN

217 "She came out swinging": David A. Lieb, "Akin Gets Conservative Endorsement, Says Sen. McCaskill Not 'Ladylike' in Mo. Senate Race," Associated Press, Sept. 27, 2012.

218 a "mom in tennis shoes": Timothy Egan, "Another Win by a Woman, This One 'Mom'," *New York Times*, Sept. 17, 1992.

218 called her performance "unbecoming": Jennifer Fenn, "No Knockout Punch, but O'Brien, Romney Duke it Out," *Lowell (Mass.) Sun*, Oct. 30, 2002.

218 referred to her as "Miss Congeniality": Paul Demko, "Minnesota Republicans Back Bills in U.S. Senate Contest," *The Legal Ledger (St. Paul, Minn.)*, May 18, 2012.

218 a "prom queen" and "Daddy's little girl": Rachel E. Stassen-Berger, "In Uphill Battle for Senate Seat, Bills is Driven to 'Stop the Debt'," *Minneapolis Star-Tribune*, Oct. 20, 2012.

218 A study of voter attitudes: Susan Page, "Study: Sexist Insults Hurt Female Politicians," *USA Today*, Sept. 23, 2010.

218 "Sexism against women in the media": Krissah Thompson, "Women's Groups Target Sexism in Campaigns," *Washington Post*, Sept. 15, 2010.

218 the formation of Name It, Change It: See the following blog posts on the Name It, Change It website: Victoria Edel, "There's Hope! Columnist Promises to Stop Fashion Policing Women in Politics," November 18, 2013; Victoria Edel, "Pink

Sneakers Are Running for Governor?," October 20, 2013; Rachel Larris, "NPR's Ombudsman Asks for Guidelines How to Describe Women Politicians," July 10, 2013.

219 Senator Klobuchar tells the story: Email from Amy Klobuchar to Claire McCaskill, May 7, 2014.

221 My colleague Kelly Ayotte: Email from Kelly Ayotte to Claire McCaskill, June 17, 2014.

224 biggest fraud in U.S. Army history: Tom Vanden Brook, "Congress Eliminates Guard's Budget for Racing; Despite Hundreds of Millions Spent, Few Potential Recruits," *USA Today*, Dec. 15, 2014.

224 Almost $3 million in bonuses: Gregory Korte, "IRS Gave Bonuses to Staff Who Didn't Pay Taxes; Almost $3 Million Went to Employees with Discipline Issues," *USA Today*, April 23, 2014.

Index

INDEX

INDEX

INDEX

About the Authors

Claire McCaskill was the first woman from Missouri elected as a U.S. senator and continues to serve in that position today. She has a BA and a JD from the University of Missouri and worked for the Jackson County prosecutor's office before she was elected to her first state legislature position in the Missouri House in 1982. She was elected Jackson County prosecuting attorney in 1992 and Missouri state auditor in 1998. She lives in St. Louis.

Terry Ganey is the author of two *New York Times* bestsellers: *Under the Influence, the Unauthorized Story of the Anheuser-Busch Dynasty* (with Peter Hernon), and *Innocent Blood, a True Story of Obsession and Serial Murder*. A finalist for the Pulitzer Prize in investigative reporting, he covered politics and government for the Associated Press, the *St. Louis Post-Dispatch,* and the *Columbia Daily Tribune.*